C000004980

Bringing the Soul Back Home

Writing in the New Consciousness

Katya Williamson

First published by O Books, 2009
O Books is an imprint of John Hunt Publishing Ltd., The Bothy, Deershot Lodge, Park Lane, Ropley,
Hants, SO24 0BE, UK
office1@o-books.net
www.o-books.net

Distribution in:	South Africa
	Alternative Books
UK and Europe	altbook@peterhyde.co.za
Orca Book Services	Tel: 021 555 4027 Fax: 021 447 1430
orders@orcabookservices.co.uk	
Tel: 01202 665432 Fax: 01202 666219	Text copyright Katya Williamson 2008
Int. code (44)	
	Design: Stuart Davies
USA and Canada	
NBN	ISBN: 978 1 84694 202 0
custserv@nbnbooks.com	
Tel: 1 800 462 6420 Fax: 1 800 338 4550	All rights reserved. Except for brief quotations
	in critical articles or reviews, no part of this
Australia and New Zealand	book may be reproduced in any manner without
Brumby Books	prior written permission from the publishers.
sales@brumbybooks.com.au	
Tel: 61 3 9761 5535 Fax: 61 3 9761 7095	The rights of Katya Williamson as author have
	been asserted in accordance with the
Far East (offices in Singapore, Thailand,	Copyright, Designs and Patents Act 1988.
Hong Kong, Taiwan)	
Pansing Distribution Pte Ltd	
kemal@pansing.com	A CIP catalogue record for this book is available
Tel: 65 6319 9939 Fax: 65 6462 5761	from the British Library.

The Women's Writing reproduced here by the kind permission of the authors. The authors assert
their moral rights that no part of the writing may be reproduced in full or part without
permission of the respective authors

Copyright Permission: From the book *The Power of Now* Copyright @1997 by Eckhart Tolle.
Reprinted with permission of New World Library, Novato, CA www.newworldlibrary.com.

Printed by Digital Book Print

O Books operates a distinctive and ethical publishing philosophy in
all areas of its business, from its global network of authors to
production and worldwide distribution.
This book is produced on FSC certified stock, within ISO14001
standards. The printer plants sufficient trees each year through
the Woodland Trust to absorb the level of emitted carbon in
its production.

Bringing the Soul Back Home

Writing in the New Consciousness

Katya Williamson

BOOKS

Winchester, UK
Washington, USA

CONTENTS

Acknowledgements

Love and gratitude to: Nani and Manono of the Ho'oli Estates Coffee Farm on the Big Island, Hawaii; Liza and Kathy of Rainbow Healing Arts, Oahu; the Holawa Street Ohana, Jennifer and Derek, particularly Bonnie Weber, and my sister Lolani, healer and visionary, without whom this final revision would not have been realized. Mahalo to all!

To the librarians of Santa Monica Library, Santa Monica, California; the guides at the Ghost Ranch library, Abiquiu; David Rasch, Carolyn Barford, Siegfried Halus, Leah Kellogg and Dano Bell of Santa Fe, New Mexico.

And most especially to those who came forward in this last revision of the book: Jan & Jeff Harris, Nancy Johnson, Helen Redman & Kenny Weissberg, Suzanne Wedow, Susan Hecht, Ann Isolde, Marilyn Sequoia & Jeffrey Laird, Veda Roubideaux, Regina & Bill O'Melveney, Stefanie Stern, Maureen & Dick Liebler and Carla Sameth: arts champions, one and all!

To Esther Kennedy for sponsoring the "Spirit of Place" writing retreats at Spirit Mountain Retreat, Idyllwild; CA and the Pisces triumvirate who helped me keep body and soul together: Bronwyn Jones, Marilyn Sequoia and Denise Helton, Bronwyn for her generosity of spirit and heart and editing prowess, whose loving help brought this book to fruition; Marilyn for her nurturing of friendship always, Denise for her intelligence, generosity of heart and sheer perseverance; David Hiemenz,, Patricia Bische, Antioch/LA faculty mentors Sharman Apt Russell and Alma Luz Villanueva; Elaine Fleming, Mary Ann Wilson , Mervat Fam, and Lynn Heinz.

To my new-found relatives, the McKell's of Stockport, their children and grandchildren, and the McRobert's of Gargrave, Yorkshire.

And especially to the Avalonians of Glastonbury: Caroline

Sherwood, Nicholas Mann, Phillipa Glasson, Colette Barnard & Green Man Ark Redwood, Seppie Hope, Carole Fox, Patricia & John Caswell, Valerie Smith, Mario Crovetto, Julie Evans, Helen Buyze, Ivona, Mano, Melanie King, Paul Leigh, Paula, John Dalton, Angela Watson, Larraine Fox, Moira & Taras of the Growing Needs Book Shop, Thelma Moeran, Liz Pearson, Elizabeth Keller, Jane Heald, Dilys Guilford, and so many others too numerous to mention, but you know how much I have appreciated experiencing "Glastonbury of the Heart" with you.

To all the luminous women writers I have worked with over the years throughout the United States, particularly in the California, Northwest, Hawaii groups, Gale Cohen, Carla Sameth, Rachel Dudek, Alicia Rowe, Carol Higgins, Veda Roubideaux, Valerie Silverio, Eileen McGruder, and Christine Eagon. Final kudos to the "Sophia's", the inspirational Glastonbury women: Maggie Stewart, Ingelise Jensen, Sabrina Dearborn, Felicity Dalton, Stacey Camfield, Pauline Royce, Jackie Crovetto, Elisabeth Tham, Jacqueline Redmond, Tamar Phoenix, Lorye Keats Hopper, Grace Bishop, Jane and Julia, among the many others.

Special thanks to John Wythe White for his editorial shape-shifting and careful scrutiny of the manuscript, Victoria Gail-White for bringing a perceptive eye to it; to Fu-Ding Cheng for the beautiful design of the book cover; to Sabrina Dearborn for her special foreword; to Stacey Camfield for the impeccable editing of the final version; to Susan Mears and Julian Robbins of the Susan Mears Agency in London for their excellent insights; and to the editors and designers of "O" Books and especially its publisher, John Hunt, for keeping alive the vision of the inner spirit and the sacred landscape.

Foreword

I am going to come right to the point: This is a remarkable book. Why? Because it does exactly what it says on the cover: enables you to write from the source within you. With a minimum amount of consistent effort, you'll get maximum results. I believe that by doing the exercises you'll develop writing that is deep, meaningful and personal, because that is exactly what happened for me.

I have completed all the exercises in this book, and most of them more than once. I started creative writing classes because I felt bottled up inside. I wanted to express my feelings in a more satisfying way and to create stories. Although I had done some writing, I wanted to draw from a deeper place and I wanted to find my real voice.

Using the "writing faster than you can think" approach, I was able to bypass my inner critic and "pleaser", and prose, poetry and memoir emerged that I was very happy with. I felt so much better being able to let my inner life flow onto the page, and even the simplest triggers opened doorways to long forgotten memories, deep insights and fresh new ideas.

I will always remember my first class with Katya. She asked us to pick a spot on the stone wall which ran alongside one length of the room and to write about it. The cynical voice inside my head kept making wisecracks like, "We've come all this way to sit here and write about the wall"?

However, the wall was only a starting point and I was duly amazed by the depth of writing that each member of our group produced, each one turning out a heartfelt piece.

In my case, I had started to describe a particular stone in the wall, and then through free association, followed a thread that enabled me to express a poignant childhood memory that I had never shared with anyone. Another woman was able to use the metaphor of the stones to describe and come to understand a hard, dispassionate part of herself, while another writer wrote at great length about her work with homeless people. That's when I discovered that this really works!

I think what distinguishes Katya's approach from other methods is that it is extremely user-friendly, and can generate profound experiences in a very simple and down-to-earth manner. The chapters each build upon one another to help create a tool box of writing skills that broaden and deepen as you move through the exercises. The text lends itself to working alone or in a group. Most importantly, it enables the writer to follow the pathways that lead to the heart of oneself.

Our spirit really can be directly accessed and experienced through our writing. Once we find that juncture where our personal self unites with the universal, we have access to a reservoir of love and wisdom that is tremendously healing. It doesn't just inform the writing, it is a source of strength and well being that adds value to the whole of our lives.

One of the most admirable qualities that Katya has as a teacher is that she is genuinely moved, touched and delighted when one of her students writes well. I take her at her word when she says that her mission in life is to empower people to write because she really, really does. Her classes are always warm and safe and conducted with a gentle guiding hand. We go at our own pace and go as deep as we want to go.

I believe that the essence of her good will, work and teaching has been translated into this book. I hope that you will enjoy the pilgrimage to your own deepest self that is on offer. Inside each of us is buried treasure, just ready and waiting to be discovered. We are all much richer than we think. I am certain that you can indeed write your soul back home.

Sabrina Dearborn
Author, *The Barefoot Book of Blessings*

Dedication To Eckhart Tolle

"Read *The Power of Now*. It's by Eckhart Tolle".

A doctor was trying to help me after the recent deaths of both of my parents. Numb from the loss, I wandered into a store and found the book and Tolles' cassettes, but couldn't quite relate to either.

A month later, struggling to merge into fast-paced L.A traffic, I pushed the cassette into the dashboard of my car as a last resort for my continuing malaise, and let his calm voice wash over me as it had done before. "What is wrong with this moment"? He said, "You can always cope with the now, but you can never cope with the future". This time, I got it!! *Be in the Moment*! The words went through my head and then coursed through my body, so simple; yet so profound. From that point on, as small moments glowed, and the sun felt good on my skin again, I knew my healing had begun.

Then, years later, when I led groups in Glastonbury and many of the writers' voices seemed to convey a deeper sense of the universal present, I knew this "living" wisdom of Tolles' was now being transmitted to them in these classes..

A further connection to Tolle soon came to light: he had lived in Glastonbury, the first place outside of the United States I had wanted to teach this writing process, feeling the energy for a new consciousness was there. It was no surprise when it then became the birthplace for this book. As he has said of sacred sites in England like Glastonbury, they hold a "unique blend of human and energetic consciousness".

Not only has my life been enriched by Tolle's level of consciousness, but I am continually impressed by how he expresses this profundity in clear and simple words. As a writer, I've been inspired by this mastery of craft, and every time I pick up his books, his teachings refresh and transform my spirit. With

many blessings, I dedicate this book to Eckhart!
Katya Williamson

Introduction

"Once the soul awakens, the search begins and you can never go back. From then on, you are inflamed with a special longing which will never again let you linger in the lowlands of complacency and partial fulfillment. The eternal makes you urgent".

Anam Cara: Spiritual Wisdom for the Celtic World, by John O'Donohue

When the largest fires in Yellowstone National Park's history gave me the opportunity to become its writer-in-residence for three summers in the 1990s, I worked with people of all ages, from all the states and twenty-six foreign countries, to help them become their own best writers. Near the juncture of three rivers at the Explorers' Museum, hundreds learned this spontaneous writing process to discover their innate ability, and when I watched their eyes light up as they reconnected to this talent, I was hooked. I knew then that I could easily and quickly bring about results for them to access their creative potential, that this brush with the eternal had indeed made them urgent.

This led me on a journey for the past sixteen years to bring workshops, retreats and classes to the western United States, England and Hawaii to help women to find their own writing voices in the same profound way I had found mine.

Then the pinnacle of this teaching that launched it into a book came two years ago while I worked with women in the land of "the Mists of Avalon", the King Arthur and Grail myths, and the Chalice Well: Glastonbury.

As I traveled back and forth from the US to the UK to lead groups on both sides of "The Pond", it was one of the women in the Sophia groups in Glastonbury who exclaimed, "I know what we're doing here! We are Writing Exercises For the Higher Self"!

When she said that, I instantly saw these words on a marquee flashing with neon lights and I knew then that a book that would more widely distribute this teaching was to be born.

You will see how the book progresses in sections marked For the Individual, The Individual in Their Environment, and the last section, Writing Exercises for the Higher Self. Ever since Thomas Moore wrote *Care of the Soul*, there has emerged a contemporary literature intrigued with the soul and its terrain. Certainly, if nothing else, a deep listening to the present is what this process strives for.

When Mother Theresa was asked how she could stand the poverty in India on a trip to the United States, she said it was less onerous than the poverty of loneliness that afflicts Western societies. This writing process is a radical means of cutting through this isolation, a rebuilding of the critical mass of self-worth within the individual that also helps them connect to others. The long-term results from this for global healing are endless.

"Where fear changes to courage, emptiness becomes plenitude, and distance becomes intimacy"
Anam Cara

A new chapter for this writing process emerged when I took my first solo pilgrimage to Glastonbury in the late 1990s after the passing of both my parents. There, as I delivered part of my mother's ashes to a place she had visited from the States, a favorite childhood location in England, near Bolton Priory in Yorkshire, a new chapter opened up for me. Soul friends emerged from Glastonbury and I realized a strong connection to the ancient lands of the west country.

Since then, six years of leading women writers on tours to sacred sites in England, to the inner circle at dawn in Stonehenge, Avebury and Cornwall, moved this spontaneous writing process to even greater heights. When we wrote for weeks at a time at the Chalice Well and the Glastonbury Abbey Retreat Houses, bridges were built between women writers from the US and UK and other members of the Glastonbury community. This eventually led to my teaching there.

Then, on a trek through Penwith Peninsula near famous Saint Michael's Mount in Cornwall (the English counterpart to Mont St Michel in Brittany), we approached the Cornish Bos-ca-wen-dun-un circle through bracken, glowing red fireweed and tall purple foxgloves. All day we had explored ancient caves (fogues), wells, and iron age forts seeing no one. But as I climbed over the last hedge to enter the circle, there was Kathy Jones, esoteric healer and one of the founders of the Goddess movement in Glastonbury, and her husband Mike. Like us, they had traveled many miles to view these stones. I thanked Mike, then editor of *Avalon* magazine, for placing in it an article describing the transformative days of my Dad's passing. We both laughed at our meeting miles away from Glastonbury in a stone circle, no less. Little did I know that this coincidence would mark the next advance in this writing process when I scheduled a session with Kathy in Southern California where we'd both be in a few weeks.

As I drove along the curving roads of Topanga Canyon above Los Angeles, I had no idea so much lay ahead in my appointment with her. When I arrived, I told her I wouldn't have been there that day in California if my English grandparents hadn't finally settled in Santa Barbara. Their odyssey from England to California was the magnetic pull for me to go back and forth between the legendary British Isles and California, with roots in both places. With this information, Kathy suggested that for the Reading the spirits of my grandparents be invited into the room to stand on both sides of me. Then she asked them. "Do you have anything to say"?

I was totally unprepared for the words that were to come from my grandfather. I had never met him; he died before I was born, but as a Chartered Public Accountant, he represented the solid practical core of the family.

"You are lucky", my grandfather's spirit had said. "You have been given the Golden Chalice. Now it will be very interesting to see what you will do with it"!

Stunned, these were the last words I ever thought I'd hear from him, or anyone, for that matter. My mind sped over a series of images: Excalibur, Cadbury, the Mists of Avalon and the parting of the veils on the sacred island. Of course, I knew the legend of the Chalice; that this receptacle that supposedly contained the blood of Jesus had been placed in the Chalice Well by his uncle, Joseph of Arimethea, who had proclaimed Glastonbury "the holiest erthe in England". When he arrived there, coming through the Bristol Channel, he had also brought a thorn tree from Jerusalem, searching for its true destination.. When he knew to put it on a hill in Glastonbury (now Wearyall Hill), that's when he identified Glastonbury as this most sacred site in England.

"What could my grandfather possibly mean"? I pondered. "How in the world could I have been given the Golden Chalice"?

A vivid memory immediately came to my mind: the smallest church in England, Culbone, in Porlock Valley on Exmoor. When I had been there the year before, little did I know it was also the site of an astonishing Temple of Light that legend had placed there in approximately 9000 BC where the light of the greatest purity had been stored, supposedly to be released at a later time for the benefit of humanity.

I wouldn't have given this legend much credence, except that, as I meditated alone in the chapel, the "invisible temple", as if in another dimension, actually rose up in front of me in an incandescent white sheen. Then I heard the words, "This is your church. Now go and find your following".

I had no idea what this structure was that had appeared to me, or what these words meant, but enthralled by its existence and beauty, I knew it had to be connected to the mystery of the special lands of England.

Out of respect, I didn't mention this to anyone for years, then learned that not only did others know of it, but they were also aware of its greater purpose: a place of eternal peace that would bring pure energy and light back to humanity. Jesus and this uncle were said to have been there. It was a sacred site that had existed for a long time in earth and water below the surface and now, as it was resurfacing, would take on the fire and air realms of communication and visibility.

"You are lucky", the spirit of my grandfather had said. "You have been given the Golden Chalice. Now it will be very interesting to see what you will do with it".

Through years of teaching this writing process, I have realized that this gift of the Golden Chalice is to be shared with others and is for all those seeking to speak the truth of their beings.

Think of bringing your own Golden Chalice, your vessel of transformation, to light. As you breathe life into your writing, and call your own unique form of expression into existence, you do so with the promise of the Chalice Well and the words of Culbone. No one in the world has the same stories or ability to tell them that you do. This is your time! The world is waiting.

MAY YOUR VOICE BE STRONG! May your heart dance with delight as you remember your passion for being and your passion for writing. I look forward to accompanying you through these pages to "*Bring Your Soul Back Home*".

WHY I RECOMMEND GROUPS FOR THIS WRITING METHOD

"Start with women's circles. Each one is like a pebble in a pond".

"The circle is an archetype that feels familiar to the psyches of most women; it is personal and egalitarian".

Jean Shinoda Bolen, *The Millionth Circle*

Bringing the Soul Back Home is for you to find your unique voice and bring your inner creativity into the light. I have found that the group format works best for this, as women not only receive support from each other but inspiration. It's a place that fosters the psyche, trust and authenticity that Bolen speaks of in this book.

A group can range from two people to twelve, or if you still prefer to work alone, your group will be a special friend or a family member who will listen supportively to you and your writing.

"What the world needs now is an infusion of the kind of wisdom women have and the form of the circle itself is an embodiment of that wisdom".

Jean Shinoda Bolen

Forge on! Here are the tools you will need to begin writing for the higher consciousness:

A group of women who are committed to the process, which involves meeting at least once a week for thirteen weeks

A room large enough to accommodate the group and private enough to avoid interruptions

Comfortable chairs or places for everyone to sit

A writing pad, preferably large and unlined

A portfolio in which you will keep all your writing throughout the course

Pencil or pen, preferably pen (no erasures necessary, doesn't need sharpening)

For each group member, a single place in their home where they will do all their writing, private enough to avoid interruptions

A timer to monitor ten-minute writing exercises

A bell to ring at the beginning and end of each session (or a candle to light and extinguish), both for the group sessions and for individual writing sessions

A CD player and a CD brought by each member of the group
(for Chapter 10 only; see the chapter for details)

Excerpt from an email about attending a "Writing for the Higher Self" Workshop in Glastonbury;

"I ended up at a creative writing group this weekend: "Writing for the Higher Self". Some gems emerged and the people there were talking of an anthology or some sort of local dramatic presentation for the work, but the material didn't feel as if it wanted to remain with the individual who had written it or even stay in the province of the select few. It was as if the words were clamouring to reach "the whole world mind" reach the "whole world mind and I don't even know exactly what I mean by that. How to explain this better?? One women spoke at the beginning of the day feeling desolate at the world situation, as important to effect any change on a world scale. How could she reach the minds of corporate America or politicians? Yet after writing one piece she said she had this inexplicable sense that something had changed because something within her had softened, opened, taken a risk and that it felt as if somehow that had influenced the whole, changed something in a subtle but radical way.

On one level it made no rational sense and yet the change was inexplicably tangible and all we had been doing was writing from the heart. That was ALL, putting our whole selves into that one simple activity. It felt very Alchemical and yet so simple and ordinary too".

JACKIE CROVETTO, GLASTONBURY

~

Section 1
The Individual

~

CHAPTER ONE

The Spontaneous Writing Process

"Writing is like the headlights of a car at night.
You can only see as far as the light shines".
E. L. Doctorow

Congratulations on your courage to be here. As you can see from this quote, you are entering into the precious realm of the Unknown. But it is precisely because this unknown is glowing with a shining potential that an excitement of an unusual kind from unharbored depths accompanies you on your path here.

In the many years of teaching this process, first to the multitudes of visitors in Yellowstone National Park, and then in numerous workshops, retreats and classes, I could sense the anticipation, then discovery, as students approached the page. I've watched potential writers be driven on by an urgency to unveil the truth of themselves and their writing. And like the car on its journey through the night, seeing as far as the headlights can shine, this disarmingly simple step-by-step process works because it illuminates and supports you all the way.

Even though you are just sitting down to read this book and do the first exercise for writing faster than you can think, it takes a courage of a deeper strength to show up at all on the page. There are many forces in the universe that support you to do this, as well as your own inner desire and longing that will lead you to who you truly are.

Whether you are a writer who wants to find a new means to revive your writing muscle, or a beginning writer, this is a powerful moment to plunge in. But don't worry, if you don't feel like plunging in, just your toe in the water is enough for now.

Find a comfortable chair in a favorite room. Hopefully, you'll be accompanied by a group of friends who will also want to undertake this process on a regular basis (weekly is preferable): the greater the number in the circle, the more potential for support. Bring with you a notebook with blank pages large enough to feel as if you can move your hands freely and flowingly across the page. Books with lines can be used, but only as long as they do not restrict your writing. Because the purpose of this exercise is to help you create as expansively as possible, write on what will give you the most freedom of movement. I have one student who scrawls across the pages in big script so she can think as clearly as possible, and it always gives her good results. Whatever feels most appropriate to you is the course of action to take, as you are the one in charge here.

Yes, you will be taking up space. This is a major goal and side effect of this unique process. Most of us, in fact, have been conditioned since early childhood to hide our light and ability. The beauty of this process is that it now announces that it is time for you, and all of us, to come out of the corners and into the space where others will hear and read our words, and in a place where they will always exist and never be taken away.

Breathe and relax in this new beginning, and realize that anything you write on this page is perfect. Take into consideration that everyone has her own unique and equally valid means of expression, and that whatever you write is your authentic mark on the world that no one else will ever create in the same way.

Breathe into your heart, and as you feel the release that comes from letting go of the stress you have unconsciously held there, rest your hand on the piece of white paper.

Feel the texture of it under your hand and skin, the pulsing between you and it. You are now part of the age-old tradition of putting pen to paper, of transmission through the written word. The fibers from the paper come from trees long ago. You are now part of a tradition where, before printing presses and technology, humans etched their impressions on the bark of trees to leave their unique stamp.

Now it is time for you (and the others) to notice the objects in this favorite room. Is there a rug that has an intriguing pattern, sheen or texture? A statue, a painting or artwork that is special? What is it made of? What are its colors? How would you describe it in detail, what does it remind you of? Is there a certain kind of light that comes through the window that is especially evocative? What memory does that bring up?

Before the next step, set your timer for ten minutes. You may mark the time on your watch but you really need a timer to help keep you focused on your writing. Let your eye scan the room, and when something jumps out, that is the moment to start moving your hand across the page.

Begin the timer and start writing faster than you can think. This means "Don't think for now". Start to write as fast as you can about what catches your attention, and let your pen go as far as your imagination will take you. Write as quickly or as slowly as you need to, and write down all the specific details you can about this object. If that rug is under your feet (always a good place to begin), how big is it? How long have you had it? You'll be surprised what other information starts to pour through, and that is the fountain from which surprising input will emerge. Just let it come without any judgment.

Please note: If you are stopped at any point, continue to write the last word again and again until you begin again. It is critical to just keep your hand moving as you write across the page.

This is the time to wake up the long dormant writing muscle.

After the ten minutes, stop writing. As this is the initial exercise for this entire writing process, you have now started up a huge engine that has tremendous force. Can you feel its power, and did you notice that, at a certain moment, something in your writing shifted on an energetic level?

You now deserve a break. Take fifteen minutes and get a glass of water or make some tea. Look out of your window, walk around for a moment, or go outside and get some sun or breathe some fresh air.

What have you discovered from this exercise? Did you move suddenly from your description of this object to another topic that became more compelling? Don't be surprised! This unexpected encounter with new material, part of the unearthing process of your unconscious, can make this happen. You have given it permission to come forward. As Clarissa Pinkola-Estes says in *Women Who Run With the Wolves*, "That which you are seeking has also been seeking you".

Take a moment and let the fact sink in that you've actually written something that might be to your liking. Congratulations! In this short time, you have probably moved thoughts, feelings, and energy that have been waiting to transform for a long time. Acknowledge that in the same way that you take a breath and take a moment to breathe into your heart.

Want to try this again? One of the most enjoyable parts of presenting this writing process is spotting people when they realize they are now on a treasure hunt, and the source of the treasure is themselves!

You never know what will emerge, but you won't find it or that part of yourself that has bee desiring to have its own voice for a long time until you seek it.

Now, choose another object in the room, and let anything that comes to mind be expressed. It is all perfect and nothing is ever wasted. Set the timer again.

Members in the groups I've conducted call this "calmly risky" writing. There is a sense of calm that comes from letting something that has longed to be heard finally emerge on the page, and the fact that there is some risk involved gives the writing a charge that pushes it to a breakthrough.

At the end of these ten minutes, give yourself and your

companions time to stop again to notice the stumbling block you've just overcome.

The journey with the "headlights" of our writing is similar to how we step into each day of our lives, and don't know what is around the corner. It's part of the fascination of being alive, and part of what is fascinating about the writing process.

To take the element of risk one step further, realize that the words that you have just written want to be heard. And that this might be the time to hear the words by sharing them out loud with the others who are accompanying you on this writing path. Be positive.

One of the reasons I advocate people reading aloud is that the words and what you write always sound different when you hear them out loud rather than when you read them to yourself.

If you are ready for this step, this is the time to introduce you to the Only Two Rules that apply to this entire process: No Disclaimers and No Judgments.

First Rule: No Disclaimers

It is important that when you start to read out loud, you don't diminish what you've done by explaining that you're not a good writer, or you weren't on top of your form at this writing or you weren't up to the exercise.

The writer is the last person to judge their own writing. In many years of teaching, I have seen that this is consistently true, so I constantly repeat these words to the groups. And, curiously enough, the members of the groups start to repeat it to each other. It doesn't matter how successful a writer may be, this urge to diminish the writing comes from the most expert to the least experienced writers. There will always be that critical voice (to be dealt with in a later chapter) that will be full of societal conditioning. Much as we wish that it weren't the case, it is part of the journey of writing.

This internal critic, who has been there for most of our lives and our attempts in writing, should have no more air time than necessary. Still, when one gets up to read our writing, there is that latent urge to slip in a comment not helpful to our performance.

DONT DO IT! This is your chance to jump off that diving board, and experience the THRILL as you land in the water, unencumbered by the old energy that has surrounded your writing for years. As you re-surface, you will have the opportunity to experience the increase in energy and self-worth this risk has given you. You deserve it! Right now, you might not believe it, but trust me, the more you read aloud, the more it will come.

If you do throw in a disclaimer the first time, don't also beat yourself up. This is hard to overcome, but eventually you will do this dive successfully.

Second Rule: No Judgments

This writing process is not about dotting the " i's" or crossing the "t's". As you use this muscle for the first time, or maybe ever, remember that whatever you are doing is perfect. The words are perfect in whatever way you say them. Allow yourself to enjoy the discovery of your writing, without those old wizened tapes that say "Why even try"? The surprise, the excavation, the unfolding of something you didn't expect: this is why it's all worth it.

The second rule, therefore, is to have no judgment about what you are writing or have written, or about anyone else's as well. It is contrary to what we've been taught in society, but this process is based on trust. It is also imperative that all members in your group (or family, friends, supporters) know that you will give each other only the most unconditional support. This safety, and good intention, is what will help all of you dive deeper into your material.

"A writer needs a sunlit place of self-regard".
Marge Piercy

You have made it through this first chapter! Congratulations are indeed in order again. Now write these words by Marge Piercy, *"A writer deserves a sunlit place of self-regard"* and put them on a special altar devoted to your own writing, a refrigerator door, or the desk where you will write. I give this quote out at the first meeting of every group, and I hope you realize the new self worth you have earned by just undertaking this process. It is one of the qualities to cultivate as a writer. You deserve and need to acknowledge how important it is to have this sunlit space of self-regard in your writing space to keep going. Preferably type or write the quote on a yellow piece of paper with the awareness that with this new experience of writing, you have just awakened the optimism to enjoy this new sunlight of your writing.

List of Exercises
- First Writing Exercise: Write faster than you can think for ten minutes. Choose a familiar object in the room that will bring up possibilities of remembering events, people, a phase of your life. Let whatever comes, come.
- Second Writing Exercise: Repeat the exercise after reading aloud what you have done in the first exercise. Choose another object in the room where you are sitting to describe.
- In the Addendum of this book are samples of stimulating writing done as "writing faster than you can think" by members of the Sophia Group in Glastonbury. Refer to them alone or with your group for further stimulation of your own writing or just a good read.

CHAPTER TWO

What Is Your Passion?

*Let yourself be silently drawn by the stronger pull of what you
really love.*
Rumi

What could be more compelling than writing about that which
you really love? That's why this chapter, as you focus on your
passions, is a favorite in this Spontaneous Writing Process.

Now that you, as the writer, have embarked on your writing
and its new beginning, you have just conquered a major obstacle
of resistance. By desiring to write, and hearing your own
authentic voice as it emerges, you have ultimately faced those
roadblocks that have stood in your way for a long time.

With the new energy you accumulate for your writing, as you
release old outmoded ways of how you perceive it, step back and
prepare to enjoy this next step of the journey. We all have
something we are passionate about that makes life worth living,
and now you will have the opportunity to revel in it with this
exercise.

Your passions could be about the smallest of things. For example,
what do you feel as you watch a dog run with great abandon across
the field or a cat as it relaxes so completely in the sun?

Or, what about food? What is appetizing about an artistically-
dressed salad, with lots of fresh vegetables? There are many such
small moments in a day to notice.

If you want to look at larger themes in your life, write about
those with whom you have made a heart commitment, or the
dreams you most want to fulfill, the nobility of a parent or the
openness of a child. The list is endless; enjoy writing about them.

Whatever you choose is perfect.

Now, write down in list form, for five minutes, faster than you can think, five people, animals, or types of activity that you are passionate about. There will be other lists. This is just the list for today that could change tomorrow, and doesn't have to reflect all of your life's experiences. Now, quickly choose one of the items on the list that most appeals to you. Set the timer for ten minutes and enjoy writing anything that you can about it.

At the core of this process, use your ability to listen deeply to yourself and your body when you embark upon this exercise. Whatever makes you more fully present is what you are striving for. It will enhance your writing.

Passion can be about anything that moves or enlivens you, like a song that touches you or the brilliant color of a flower. Do you remember the cup of coffee the angel describes in the movie "Wings of Desire"? In his first morning as a human, he evokes the smell of it so vividly that one becomes happy just to be alive on this planet. This is the kind of openness that would be good to allow now in your writing.

If other trains of thought arise, let them take you where you need to go. If you start to write about a passion and a larger idea enters your mind and pen, follow it. This is the time to listen to what comes up, since it is all gold below the surface of your consciousness that has waited a long time to become more visible. This is your moment to realize what is fulfilling in your life, and what you have gratitude for, through your writing.

Clarissa Pinkola Estes, a Jungian analyst, talks about the act of writing as a hook that we let down into the river of our unconsciousness, and that we never know what kind of fish we might pull up. Her theory is that this river flows all the time, and even when we don't write, this underground source and strength of ours is there.

I can feel the relief in the groups when I've described this concept, as most people who have an abiding interest in writing may not have been able to engage in it as often as they wanted to.

You don't have to be responsible to keep the river going. It is always there. Today you just have to allow yourself to lower the hook of intent to write into this vastness, and to see, maybe just out of curiosity, what kind of fish comes up. Nothing is lost, and all material is important.

These first pages you have written are words on paper. Later, you will begin to see the emergence of the themes in your life that are especially for you in your life to write about. So be watchful for the gems that might already be coming forth.

THE *TEMENOS*

It is important to mention right now as you go in and out of your writing space that you are also entering a kind of sacred space. As you start, in theory at the same time every day, every couple of days, or at least once a week, know that it is important that it be at a regular time.

What occurs is the creation of a kind of special sanctuary for your self and your writing (and anyone else who is doing this with you). The Greeks called it *temenos*, and I first heard this concept when I read *Crossing To Avalon* by Jean Shinoda Bolen. In the same context in which she uses it, it honors you and your writing as you commence with these writing exercises, and that you are in a new space of consciousness and concentration. You applaud yourself for showing up on the page, and anyone else who accompanies you on this journey. Each time you start to write, each time you read your work or listen to others read theirs, in this deep listening space, you are in a *temenos*.

When you finish the exercises and close the session, know that you now close this *temenos* that surrounds you, and you will come out into a different place in your daily life. Perhaps it would be useful at this time to light a candle or ring a bell when you begin each session. It's good to have this way to indicate that a change is occurring in your surroundings as you immerse yourself in the writing. When you finish the session, blow out the candle or ring the bell again.

This process is a quest into your own special creative development, and needs demarcation when you come in and out of the experience.

Remember there are numerous guides that support you, especially when this seems new. The more you experience it, the more natural this *temenos* and its boundaries will become. As Brenda Ueland, one of the first teachers in the United States in the 1930s who relished the spontaneous creative writing results of her students, said:

"Why should we all use our creative power and write or paint or play music? Because there is nothing that makes people so generous, lively, bold and compassionate. Because the best way to know Truth or Beauty is to try to express it. And what is the purpose of existence but to discover Truth and Beauty and to share it with others"?

WELCOME TO THE TEMENOS!

Now to begin again. Have you finished the first item on your list of passions in a ten-minute time frame? Then choose another on the list, set the timer again and learn about why you feel so passionate about it while you write for ten more minutes.

After completing this second exercise, as you feel brave, read to the others what you have written. All of you should take a turn. In this deep listening process, you will hear what the writing sounds like.

What have you discovered about yourself and your writing from these exercises? Were there any unexpected surprises? What were they? Discuss this with friends and writing companions.

From a structural point of view, the writing from this list of five passions can be done in one sitting. Or, in a week's time, you can write about a passion a day and then the next time you get together, read your results to each other.

All of this material you have written so far will be useful to you, and can be utilized for exercises in later chapters.

As you embark upon these exercises for Chapter Two, keep in mind this word that a writing friend, from our Los Angeles Writing Group that met for over ten years every Thursday night in Venice, and I would say when we took another writing step: "Corragio" (have courage)!

CORRAGIO!

List of Exercises

- First Writing Exercise: Write a list of five things you are passionate about, from small to big, in five minutes. Make notes on why you have chosen these five items.
- Second Writing Exercise: Choose one in particular that catches your eye and write for ten minutes about that.
- Third Writing Exercise: Choose another item on the list and write about it faster than you can think for another ten minutes.
- Read whatever you choose out loud to your writing companions. Remember that you are supported by them.
- Refer to the examples of these writing exercises in the Addendum, either by yourself or with your group.

CHAPTER THREE

Become More Present in Your Writing:
EXPLORING THE BODY AND ITS SENSES

"As soon as you honor the present moment, all unhappiness and struggle dissolve, and life begins to flow with joy and ease. When you act out of present-moment awareness, whatever you do becomes imbued with a sense of quality, care and love even the most simple action".
Eckhart Tolle

Before we begin this chapter, please remember that this writing process, *writing faster than you can think*, is disarmingly simple. All you need to do is recognize that there is a wealth of experience at your fingertips, and your act of sitting down with pen, paper, and a willingness to be present is a sign that you have everything you need right here, right now. Begin.

Have you thought about what a miracle your body actually is? Now that you've put hand to paper and heard the beginnings of your own voice, as well as recognized what you feel passionate about and how that can ignite your writing, let's go to this next source of inspiration.

As if you are an archaeologist, unearthing the layers of your being, we will now take a look at the body: the home of an infinitesimal number of electric synapses, the juncture of equally as many muscles, cells, bones and organs. The body is fertile ground for the writing to take off in several directions.

Sit down with your paper and begin to write (after you set the timer for ten minutes) about a part of your body. Write about it as if you are looking down on it from an overview perspective. Does a single part of it jump out? Or is there a concept you have long waited to write about, such as the pressures society has put on all of us to have the perfect body? This is a time to rant and rave, if you want. I've been impressed with how much writing immediately comes from this topic, and since it is indeed a search for the truth of our beings, then what can be more immediate than our bodies to work from?

Eckhart Tolle says in *The Power of Now* and *The New Earth* that by our "deeply listening" to our bodies instead of being run by our minds, we will understand the essence that gives human beings the huge potential to create. This spontaneous writing process involves deep listening to understand this greater potential.

"The atoms that make up your body were once forged inside stars, and the causes of even the smallest event are virtually infinite".
Eckhart Tolle from *The New Earth*

When you are ready to go onto the next exercise, after this first one of writing faster than you can think about the body from an overview, turn the timer on again.

Write about it from the smaller scale perspective for the next ten minutes. Is there some little part of your body that has always fascinated you, but you don't know exactly why? This is the time to unravel that puzzle.

For instance, as I prepared to lead a recent writers' retreat in Idyllwild, in the mountains above Palm Springs, California, I looked at my left wrist and noticed that the vertical blue vein curving diagonally from left to right across it was more prominent than the one on my right wrist. "What is the purpose of that blue vein"? I thought, and then realized I had to write about it because I knew some compelling imagery would come from it.

27

"Why is it blue"? was the next thought, and "What is the difference between left and right wrists"? These are the kinds of questions that you can also ask yourself that will lead to unexpected discoveries. What better time is there than now to contemplate our bodies before injuries or illness? Take this time to honor your being, and what makes you unique.

If you've ever had a broken bone and watched the body's cells and nutrients rush in to heal it, there's a new awareness of how efficiently and tenderly the body takes care of us. Can you write about when you remember an instance in your life that your body demonstrated this true value? Begin for a ten-minute write.

I partially answered the earlier question about the blue vein: "I write with my left hand, hence the raised blue vein, but even so I am still curious as to why it is that shade of blue. Why am I so attracted to that particular shade"?

This curiosity can lead your writing towards a multitude of possibilities and take you into unexplored territory you never dreamed of. Be prepared for dramatic responses that may uplift or unsettle you, but will never be dull.

"The body itself is a screen to shield and partially reveal the light that's blazing inside your presence"
Rumi

After you finish this exercise, and have read it out loud to the others, let's go now on to the next tier of "writing that looks at our existence".

Since quite a few of us live in urban settings, it is even more important to access the present through the senses, especially if you are constantly exposed to the hectic pace of crowds walking, running, speeding cars, sirens and cell phones everywhere. If you have been surrounded by this over-stimulation, allow these writing exercises and the process of writing to help you regain your natural state of essential calm.

When you have stopped to look at any flower in this environment, have you noticed the difference in contrast (from the urban center) to its stationary peace? How often have you taken the time to sit for a few moments to allow yourself to feel the heat of the sun on your skin? Something as simple as this brings a variety of possibilities for writing.

"Use your senses fully. Be where you are. Look around. See the light, shapes, colors, textures. Be aware of the silent presence of each thing. Be aware of the space that allows everything to be. Listen to the sounds; don't judge them. Listen to the silence underneath the sounds. Touch something, anything, and feel and acknowledge its Being. Observe the rhythm of your breathing; feel the air flowing in and out, feel the life energy inside your body".
Eckhart Tolle

As an exercise, please re-read this quote again, slowly, and out loud. On another sheet of paper, writing faster than you can think, describe what this life energy in your body feels like. Just for the fun of it, for the experience of it, try to listen to the silence beneath the sounds that he has mentioned to help you with your response. Listen. Listen again. Feel, then write. Let this inner body that you just wrote about, lead you into the writing.

Now you are even more ready to relish the senses. There is a delicious mixture of touch, taste, smell, hearing and seeing that surrounds you as you read this. Can you imagine your life without any of them? Before you start the next exercises, breathe again.

For the next ten-minute exercise, let's take **taste**. Do you remember something that was salty, tangy, sweet, bitter or tart? What does it remind you of, who was with you? Allow yourself a minute to let the images flow through you, giving a background description of where you were when you had this experience.

29

Was it a luscious piece of fruit whose juices dripped all over you as you ate it? A hot barbecue sauce, or the hot horseradish that goes with sushi that brought tears to your eyes?

After the timer goes off, and you and your companions have read to each other, try something a little more difficult to write about: the sense of **smell**. It is one of the hardest to describe in words, but you can write around it, if need be. As in "Wings of Desire", the description of the coffee by the Angel was good enough for the audience to experience how tantalizing the smell of the coffee can be. Sometimes that's all that needs to be put into words.

Challenging as it might seem, smell is also the most evocative sense since it immediately takes you back to the source, however old you were at the time. So you could write about your mother's perfume or your grandmother's lavender sachet, the hint of soap on someone's collar, the smell of a meal when you were really hungry, the smell of pine trees in the forest and that deeply textured smell of wood. Can you now begin to see that there are many writing themes you've had within you for a long time that have been waiting to come forward?

One of the participants at the Spirit Mountain retreat came strikingly close to describing the sense of smell:

"There is a fragrant, cool
smell to morning dawn,
it is the smell of the earth
and moist leaf green
not yet made pungent
by the heat of the sun"

from Rachel Dudek's poem
"Morning at Spirit Mountain"

"There's something about the smell of these tall red-crested Jeffrey Pines", I wrote in California, "as if it goes into and comes from somewhere deep in the earth in the silence of these standing trees. It's what has brought me back time and again to these mountains, but I still don't know what that essence is".

As Tolle explains in *The Power of Now*, it's not the what or why of our lives that maximizes our moment-by-moment existence; it's how we perceive our lives and the situations we find ourselves in on a daily level. This how is often best defined through an immediate experience of these senses, and as we tend them, our creativity begins to sparkle.

Sight: From the first moment we wake up to the last sight we have when we go to bed, the retinas and lenses of our eyes are miraculously designed to make constant adjustments for us to see what we are looking at. For the next ten minutes, write about: "What is one of the most beautiful sights you've ever seen?"

The anatomy of eyesight is to look outward, and that stretches our energy outside of ourselves, whereas this writing process is about looking inward, to help you see with an inner sight.

Begin with a simple description of this beautiful scene with its colors, forms, contours. Then describe why it was so special to you. You can keep a separate list of memorable experiences of sight, and write about them when you feel the urge. If you want, describe a sunset that was particularly special: write about the clouds and the color of the sky. Isn't it amazing that one moment it is gold and blazing, and takes all our attention, then, quietly, at the last moment, it slips with quiet grace beyond the horizon somehow like what it is to be alive, present one day here, then gone. Write about that, too, if you want.

Then, the next exercise: "Why is the gift of sight so significant to you"?

By now, you will hopefully be getting the sense of the rhythm for pacing these exercises. If you and your companions would like, take a day to write about them at your own desk, or write three in a one-day session together, and then come back in a week to share them. It's for you to decide. The main point is to do these exercises consistently, within a week's period of time, preferably, so that by the time you finish the last chapter, number thirteen, you will have been involved in this writing process for a quarter of the year. That is a solid amount of time for you to distinguish the themes that keep recurring in your writing that will make up the body of your work. It will also give time for you to identify your unique writing voice and style.

The deep satisfaction that comes when you write on a consistent basis with others is that you will begin to hear each other's voices as well as your own. Those voices will be so strong that, even if you don't see each other for a long time, when you begin to read from your writing again, you will recognize them. Each voice will be like an intrinsic part of your world. It will be as close to you as a friend you will never lose. That's how profound your writing can be to you and others.

"There's a huge stillness here, I can hear bat's wings around me; peoples' voices travel over long distances, like the sounds from the coyotes last night". .Another vignette about sound from the mountains where the Jeffrey pines were. **The sense of hearing**. There is so much that can be said about how sound helps us to bypass the endless tapes that rattle around in our thinking.

Sit under a wind chime and hear its prayer pushed by the wind, and then write about how that calms you, makes you more peaceful. Have you ever heard a gong tap a Tibetan bowl and all thought is immediately lost? That is peace. "What memorable time did you hear bells or gongs ringing"? Set the timer and listen to the sounds you hear right now. Write about them. Are they loud? Soft? Jarring? Soothing? Whatever they are, by your attention to them, you'll learn about yourself in greater detail.

Is there a night when you heard the sounds of a summer concert as dusk hovered around you, while you were in green gardens? What was that like? Possibly you can describe how each of the instruments sounded while how the dusk changed its color.

More Ideas: Does your family have a story about how you listened to music together and the music you heard brought you closer? What about the sound of waves as they hit the shore? What do they evoke? Another possible exercise as a last exercise: What has been one of the most difficult things you've ever heard? What did it mean to you? Why?

Take time to read out loud what each person has, by now, most likely been itching for everyone to hear. It's amazing how fast this turnaround can be. One minute, you think you could never read out loud. The next, it becomes imperative that you share it because you know you'll hear it in a different way. And this is also a way to receive constructive feedback. Constructive is the operative word here: there will be more on this in another chapter, but in this process, think of giving feedback as "what this piece brings up for you". It is important the conversation stay on the level of curious inquiry and support, and is not about grammatical or style issues.

Touch, the last sense to write about, envelops the essence of skin and a tactility special to being human. Have you ever had a massage or simply touched someone's shoulder with a message and realized how far beyond words the touch took you? Touch, like smell, is potentially easier to write about when comparing it to other elements.

"The air is soothingly soft,
like an emollient.
It bathes me in the morning coolness
of a silent, earth-hugging breeze
that doesn't stir the trees"

from Rachel Dudek's poem
"Morning at Spirit Mountain"

Choose something tactile to write about: a strand of hair, how it
has so many colors when the sun catches it in a certain light. What
does that symbolize about the meaning of that person to you? Or,
as another idea, the remembrance of a certain tree from
childhood. How did its bark feel to your touch? What was its
texture like? How did it feel to you as you climbed its branches ñ
strong, supple? And possibly a more recent experience: How sand
feels as you walk along a beach and. its color and texture? Did you
sink into it and or feel a special quality of softness from it?

SUGGESTION: These exercises can be covered over a period of
weeks, with writing about one sense per week at a designated
regular time during the day. Then meet with the group to trade
stories and writing pieces. Or, if you're so inclined with your
group, do more than one sense in a three-hour time span with
each other. That's usually enough time to write, share and read.
You'll be surprised at the depth that you will go to together.

Writing about the senses touches us more deeply than we
realize, and I have seen this happen over and over again in the
classes.

As the psychoanalyst Rollo May said: "What is it about
writing? Isn't it just putting two words, then two sentences
together? No, it is nothing less **than forging in the smithy of one's
soul**".

By now, notice the portfolio of writing you are compiling and the patterns of writing styles that are emerging. Everything is material. The exercises you have just done have added to it. A special note is important at this time: some of this output may have seemed surprisingly easy to write, since it was just below the surface waiting to be unearthed for a long time. It actually can be some of the best writing that will come forward, even though it has seemed to happen so effortlessly.

It is no small feat what you have been doing in these three chapters! What has come through in this short period of time is a preview of what is to come. Remember to respect the depth that you are plumbing as it will continue to lead you on to even greater writing, *forging in that smithy of your soul.*

"Only if we are still enough inside and the noise of thinking subsides can we become aware that there is a hidden harmony here, a sacredness, a higher order in which everything has its perfect place and could not be other than what it is you can sense it when you let go of thought, become still and alert, and don't try to understand or explain. As soon as you sense that hidden harmony, that sacredness, you realize you are not separate from it, and when you realize that, you become a conscious participant in it".
Eckhart Tolle, *The New Earth*

List of Exercises
- First Writing Exercise: Write about a part of the body by using an overview perspective of your body. For ten minutes, write, if your writing companions want to read, take time for each of you to share. Please remember that the bottom line is to be supportive.
- Second Writing Exercise: Write for ten minutes about an experience where you remember an instance in your life when your body demonstrated to you its true value.

- Third Writing Exercise: Write for ten minutes about a smaller part of your body, preferably one you haven't noticed before. What does it indicate? What is it? Look at it with curiosity, and write for ten minutes.
- Fourth Writing Exercise: For ten minutes, write about one of the senses **taste** in all its facets and what it means.
- Fifth Writing Exercise: For ten minutes, write about **smell** and other memories or images that smell conjures up for you. In the same way, the following exercises will unearth for you nuggets of gold of information that you will be using in later parts of this process.
- Sixth Writing Exercise: Write for ten minutes about **sight** and read.
- Seventh Writing Exercise: Write for ten minutes about **hearing** and read.
- Eighth Writing Exercise: Write for ten minutes about **touch** and read.
- By yourself or with your group, refer to the examples of these writing exercises in the Addendum.

~

Section 2

The Individual in Her Environment

~

CHAPTER FOUR

Nature as the Spirit of Place in Your Writing

"I sit at the base of this tree trunk, sinking a taproot from my
tailbone. Like a straw, it draws up from mother earth the dark,
rich, sustaining blood of embodiment".
Joan Zerrien, Idyllwild, California

As we move from the chapter on our senses in writing, let's take them with us to explore the larger body of nature that also sustains us on this earth.

While you look at nature around you, take one of the senses we wrote about (an element of water, fire, air or earth) and combine it with this part of nature. For instance, how does that favorite body of water you live nearby look with your eyesight? What does the smell of smoke from a campfire you once sat around evoke? Do you remember hearing the sound of a coyote or some other animal over long distances? Or sinking your root into mother earth at the base of a tree? What did the touch of the bark feel like on your skin?

I know you are adept at making your writing elastic. As you play with your imagination, remember this special event of being alive with nature, and let it enfold you in your writing as you put pen to paper for ten minutes.

After you finish, and read your offerings to your colleagues, I'd now like to share with you some of my own inspirations from the oldest national park in the world, Yellowstone, the same size as Switzerland or the state of Delaware. As if seen from a distance, here is the "Poem to the Lake":

"Suddenly from the plane window the Lake,
like a glove thrown loosely over the landscape,
platinum and silver,
a hand resting on the earth"

The largest inland lake in the continental United States was seen from a great distance. What have you seen or heard from a similar distance in nature? And what was your reaction? Wherever the images are held in the backwaters of your memory, now is the time to bring them to the surface in your writing. As the second exercise, please write for ten more minutes, about this experience and how, for instance, a favorite seascape, a train whistling through a mountain, or smoke over distant terrains in the forest (or anything else unique to you) created an impact. As you share this writing and your experiences with others, watch for any changes in style, timbre, or resonance in your writing voice. Please remark on them as positively as you can with each other (no disclaimers).

Let's now take the opposite close-up lens, and record nature with one of the senses as if it is right in front of your face

From my poetry collection as a writer-in-residence, *Shards of Yellowstone* (using sound) in "Burial Site at Biscuit Basin":

"Behind the burial site
of a lost animal,
a geyser constantly bubbles"

(Or using sight) in "The Leave Taking":

"As always, the air was porous, cool and steamy
There they stood, silently tamping their feet.
Not one, not two, but fifteen buffalo just across the road,
steam from their noses,
with half-lidded eyes"

Nature stimulates our deepest stirrings of creativity. Allow yourself to remember the freedom you once knew as a child in nature, and speed your words across the page like you used to run at that age in this close-up writing exercise. Well done. Now, give yourself a break. Walk around, have a glass of water, and feel the energy coming back into your body.

How lucky we are that writing is fueled by the imagination, and nature, in its essence, opens us with great exuberance to this imagination. Now that you've expanded and contracted your writing and experience of the senses, let's allow the deeper wellsprings of your childhood to support you now.

"What is the first time you remember interacting with nature as a child? Anything goes. Tomorrow it could be a different perception. For today, writing faster than you can think, what was it? And what did it mean to you? Nature for me has always been a source of communion and solace in alone time.

My first moment of remembered interaction was connecting with a grove of green bamboo in Monterey, California, outside Navy quarters. It was a place of respite that surrounded me in peace and comfort. I know I'll write about it more to understand why it made such an impact. That's the beauty of writing: it will constantly give you new information and inspiration, particularly in instances when you go back over those moments where nature served as a reservoir for your spirit and your writing.

"Nature is made to conspire with spirit to emancipate us"

These words are from a favorite poet, Ralph Waldo Emerson, leader in the Transcendentalist Movement in the United States in the 1800s.

Think for a moment about similar poets who revered nature and have inspired you. Find some of their words to refuel your writing, and let yourself be inspired.

Now, we will approach nature in a more mythic way through an exercise designed to help you expand your writing voice by trying out dialogue. Our task is to write about the turn of the seasons, spoken in the special voice of that season. Choose a season that will soon be changing to a new one and speak with its voice, and how it feels about ending. Then speak with the new season's voice in reply as this persona begins, and see what emerges. This exercise was a favorite of the Sophias, and I'm sure once your try your hand with it, it will be one of yours too.

Like pictographs tracing markings made by humans in caves throughout time, writing is an imprint. Realize that you may never know who will be affected by yours, or when they will read your work, but once you have put it out there into the world, others will be impacted by it. It may be in a few years or in a few decades: you will never know. That's one of the special parts of becoming the writer that you are!

List of Exercises
- First Writing Exercise: Write for ten minutes about an aspect of nature as experienced by one of the senses.
- Second Writing Exercise: Write for ten minutes about something you have you seen, heard, or smelled from a similar distance in nature. What was your reaction? How did it create an impact? As you share this writing with others, watch for any changes in style, timbre, or resonance in your writing voice.
- Third Writing Exercise: Write for ten minutes using the opposite close-up lens, and record nature with one of the senses as if it were right in front of your face. Allow yourself to remember the freedom you once knew as a child in nature, and speed your words across the page like a fast-flowing river for this close-up writing exercise.
- Fourth Writing Exercise: Write for ten minutes about the first

time you remember an interaction with nature as a child. Anything goes. What was it and what did it mean possibly to you?

- Fifth Writing Exercise: Write for ten minutes about the turn of the seasons, spoken in the special voice of a season. Choose a season that will soon be changing and speak with its voice, and how it feels about ending. Then speak with the new season's voice in reply as this persona begins, and see what emerges! This is an opportunity to write about nature in a mythic way.
- By yourself or with your group, refer to the examples of these writing exercises in the Addendum.

CHAPTER FIVE

The Sanctuary of Your Writing

"The time will come
when with elation
you will greet yourself arriving
at your own door,
in your own mirror,
and each will smile
at the other's welcome"
Derek Wolcott, *Soul Flares*

"The destination is the journey, and the journey is the destination" is
an old Celtic saying that implies that the journey you are undertaking is already bringing you the seeds of your arrival.

This is why it is critical at this time that you create a protective
space around yourself for your muse and your writing, your own
temenos. Honoring this significant step that you've initiated to
become aware of your inner strength and resources through this
process, imagine an oasis where your writing can occur. Only you
know what that haven should contain for you to feel comfortable
and at ease, and this chapter is dedicated to help you discover
this. Here are two personal tales of sanctuaries:

West Los Angeles, California:
One long-term writing immersion in my adult life was writing on
a desk made of blond wood in the corner of a large room. I would
stare out at the heavily painted turquoise steps of the adjoining
adobe building, soft yellow-white buds of the cottonwood tree
across from my window, red geraniums or camellias in pots
below.

My psyche and body knew I would be there every morning around 9 a.m., give or take a few minutes, and I would watch the seasonal changes of these trees, plants and birds to the point that they became part of the writing. As Jim, the ninety-two-year-old landlord of the white duplex of California cottages would repaint the steps with yet another coat of turquoise, I would add another layer of depth to my writing. It didn't matter why he was driven to do it, or why I was sitting at my desk, but we shared this moment of re-creation together.

Sometimes small birds would pick up tiny filaments of plastic off the slanted roof to build nests in the cottonwood at springtime, and classical music would softly patter in the background, like a water fountain. Despite busy LA streets only a couple of blocks away, this room held a silence, and in that meditation, the writing went deep.

My reward would be a long beach walk at sunset between the Santa Monica and Venice piers, where I'd continue my solitary thinking about the writing, and watch the last impressionistic arcs of purple and blue light on the sand after the sun went down.

As you set the timer for ten minutes, what are some of those other writing times where you sat down and wrote on a regular basis that come forward? What are the particulars you relished about them? When you remember these instances in your writing, what did you like most about your surroundings? Now, use your writing to envision your desk and surroundings. What would most stimulate your creativity? Dig deep; let your imagination go to all the corners of possibility. What does the space that helps you to expand your confidence while equally nurturing you look like? Use your writing to dream with, if you can't picture this sanctuary yet.

After you write for ten minutes, please share these visions out loud with the others, and listen to each other's essays. Now, just to turn the tables a bit, one of you read out loud the following while the others close their eyes to meditate on a Sophia's words from Glastonbury:

Glastonbury, Somerset, England

"I am sitting at the table in the kitchen. It's 7:15 a.m., the boiler is purring, the clock is ticking and I can hear footsteps above me as someone potters to the bathroom. I have just lit a squat, white pillar candle that sits in a crockery bowl in the centre of the table. The first one up in our house always does this to welcome in the House Angel for the day.

The kitchen is one of my writing places. It is where I usually sit in the morning on school days before my daughter wakes up. I sit and write either before or after I make her packed lunch. It is relatively quiet here, and cozy.

I love my kitchen. When I sit and write here, I am calm, relaxed and centered yet I am also in Mom mode, alert and listening. I listen for the sounds of my daughter and husband getting up, the water running in the bathroom, all the signs that the day is beginning in earnest. When I write in my kitchen I am the heart and the hearth of my home. I am the Mother of the World".

Sabrina Dearborn

In the same way you described objects in the room in the first chapter, please write in detail about what special objects, such as Sabrina's candle, you would like to have in this sanctuary that would give you the visual and psychic support to continue.

Sabrina writes:

"Although it has changed shape and size many times, a candle has always sat there since our family was formed. It is the light that travels with us wherever we go. It has been with us when we moved from flat to flat in London, then to our home here in Glastonbury.

45

It is the Light that reminds us that a greater Love and playfulness is at the heart of all life, no matter what conflicts or resolutions we experience together".

What are the items you would most need for your *temenos* in a similar way, an altar space that will enable you to write? Please make a list, and choose one to write about that most affects you now. How does it fit into your envisioned writing space?

After ten minutes, and after you read your pieces to each other, fill in the blanks of what additional items you'd want in the space: photographs, art objects, vases of water. After the timer sounds, please read this out loud to your companions.

Sabrina writes:

"Millie, a white fluffy cat with a Siamese-like face, has just walked across my notebook and sits regally beside my pad as if presiding over the writing that will follow.

The safety and security of these early morning moments, the promise of the day as I sit catching up with myself from the night and bringing myself back from sleep through the writing. In a moment I will stretch like the cat has begun to do. I want to make sure that my body still fits after my nightly travels, and then I will make my daughter's lunch".

You have now put in place the success for your writing to unfold.

And we come to a profound aspect of writing. It takes up space that will not be relinquished. It can never be cast aside. We come from generations and societies where many had to, on a regular basis, give up their space for others, and sometimes were told it was selfish. Now is the time for the change to occur! Every writer who determines she will write must have the opportunity to not only be heard, but to have the assurance it is permanent.

Now is the time for your writing to be heard. It will go out in the world and occupy space that will not be taken away or pushed back into the corners. Wake up your writer! Celebrate!

And remember, as you enter your special sanctuary, a whole tribe of writers are around you who carry you forward. They support you in every possible way. You are a part of something larger than yourself in this writing and with your muse.

List of Exercises

- First Writing Exercise: Write for ten minutes about your memories of writing times that come forward, and the particulars you relished about them. Include images that you would like to play with to envision your desk and surroundings. Imagine the most expansive and equally nurturing space for you.
- Second Writing Exercise: Write for ten minutes about the special objects, such as Sabrina's candle, that you would like to have in your sanctuary that would give you visual and psychic support. Make a list and then choose the one to write about that most affects you.
- Third Writing Exercise: Write for ten minutes about additional items you'd want in your space: photographs, art objects, vases of water.
- By yourself or with your group, refer to the examples of these writing exercises in the Addendum.

CHAPTER SIX

Calmly Risky Writing

"There are some deep depths out there".
Yogi Berra

That's why this method of writing in the new consciousness has been dubbed as 'calmly risky'.

For this is the point: At one moment we head to the diving board to stand at the edge, and wait for our turn to plunge in, head-first into the writing. But, at the same time, we instinctively know, to do our most expansive work we must be safe.

With this method, you are in control of both the action of your movement forward in the writing and your re-action as well. For the need to find the comfort zone parallels your growth.

I can almost automatically say that most groups, in the middle of this process, will arrive at the beginning of the sessions excited to read the writing they've done during the week, while gritting their teeth at the same time when they get up to read.

It's a natural reaction. All of us who've used this process over time still hold on tight because the method, by its very essence, creates a kind of exposure. It's the kind of exposure that is thrilling and can sometimes seem daunting at the same time. We are conditioned to protect ourselves as we grow up in this society to not show any vulnerability.

"What will people think"? is the question that immediately arises. But, then, when we understand the no disclaimers and no judgment rules that finally get under the skin after just doing it, doing that dive, groups start saying those words to each other, "no disclaimers" and laughingly urge each other on. "Calmly risky writing" becomes a banner of courage we quote to each other, and this one-part adrenalin, one-part comfort is the hallmark of the practice that brings about such successful results.

Now that you have created your sanctuary (Chapter Five) and a support team for your writing, allow a little more of this adrenalin to percolate through your being. Remember, "there are some deep depths out there", and they are waiting for you as much as you have been waiting for them to appear.

I repeat this here because, as you go deeper into this process, it is sometimes normal to forget why you had a strong desire to write in the first place. As we further activate our unconscious, it doesn't want us to undergo this step forward or maybe there is too much change, too much risk. But wait a minute, what is that wisdom we constantly hear throughout our days that 'the only thing constant in life is change'?

Try this experiment now: Stand up and place your feet firmly on the ground or floor. Feel the energy as it comes up your legs for one long moment.

Then touch your hands to your toes, and let all that you've taken in flow down your arms and legs, to be absorbed in the earth or floor you stand on.

Now, feel the energy come back up from beneath you, and take these words into your whole being: "When you become conscious of being, what is really happening is that being is becoming conscious of itself". Eckhart Tolle, *The Power of Now*.

Stand a moment longer, feel the texture of the earth or floor again, and sit down. Feel refreshed? With the others, take out your pen and paper and, writing faster than you can think, write what happened when you read this penetrating quote. What are the first glimmers of images coming to you?

After ten minutes, read your writing out loud to each other. Now you're ready for more calmly risky writing.

But before we can commence, it is necessary to address one of the biggest obstacles that keeps us from our best and truest writing. Conditioned by all sorts of misfired messages from growing up in a critical society, the critic has been blown out of proportion. It's a challenge to whittle it down from the bad-boy status it can hold over many the writer, and put it into proper perspective.

One powerful antidote is from the funny account written in *Bird by Bird* by Anne Lamott, one of the best writers on writing because she incorporates humor into it so well.

A writer in the throes of writer's block, undone by her own critic, goes to her therapist. The therapist suggests that she visualize all those who have told her she had no artistic talent throughout the years with their jaws in a glass bottle wagging. The writer only needs to open the lid of the bottle occasionally to hear the noise that comes from the trapped critics, and then to drop the lid again.

What an ingenious way to put this too serious issue of the critic into perspective. Try it sometime. It's more than effective. You are in control. And to weather part of being a writer, you do eventually have to come to terms with the fact that the critic will always accompany you. It comes with the territory, but it is your choice to allow its volume to be high or low, and to recognize how serious or funny you want to make it.

"You get your intuition back when you make space for it", Anne Lamott writes, "when you stop the chattering of the rational mind. The rational mind doesn't nourish you. You assume it gives you the truth, because the rational mind is the golden calf that this culture worships".

Now it's your opportunity to turn the tables! For the next ten minutes, write anything and everything you'd like to say to this buffoon of a critic. Use swear words if you want, lots of exclamation points, and write in bold capitol letters. Tell your critics, through your lifetime, how they never helped you, never gave you a chance, even though you deserved so much better. Remember from a long time ago when the criticism first started, and in an effort to release once and for all that which no longer serves you, or isn't even real anymore, tell these critics everything you can about how they made you feel, and remember to breathe.

After ten minutes of writing, pause, breathe, and go for a glass of water. Get some air outside. How has this writing and then your release of this critic made you feel? You've done it! Bravo!

With the same gusto you brought to the above exercise, on another page, for ten more minutes, write about "How might this critic have helped me in some way"? This may seem preposterous, but when you go a layer deeper down in your writing, this information may help you realize a whole new perspective.

At the end, write "I am grateful to you, critic, for ....." and list three items. Since writing in gratitude is an empowering experience, these exercises will help you gain insight and strength to get along with the live-in critic better.

Now, read your words to your companions, and note how you all feel about the two different exercises, and bring this topic back into balance into your life.

Since your comfort zone may have been pushed to the limit, to as far to the edge of the diving board as you might want to go, remember that Anne Lamott finishes with, "You get your confidence back by being militantly on your own side; don't look at your feet to see if you're doing it right. Just dance"!

Now that you've confronted another imaginary fear, your desire and ability to write will not only be emboldened, but you will be on the solid ground of having passed through another gateway and weathered this particular storm. Congratulations!

Let's go back and review what have been the highlights so far in your writing. Please pick up the pen and address: What have been some unexpected highlights in my writing so far? What, in small quiet moments, have I been pleasantly surprised by? What was unexpected? Please write for ten minutes about these questions, and also be aware of how you feel about these changes in your awareness of your work.

After you've read this out loud and shared it with the others, now circle some words where you sensed a nerve ending, and a certain charge that came through you as you wrote them. They will be some of the most significant teachers to you of what your writing wants to tell you.

Understand this, and you will be well on your way in this path of your writing.

Take a separate sheet of paper and start a list of these special words that you will add to throughout the entire experience. These phrases or words will act like a string of beads, and serve as your lifeline to your authentic writer self.

YOU HAVE MADE IT THIS FAR. NOW DON'T GIVE UP!

List of Exercises
- First Writing Exercise: Stand up and feel the energy as it comes up your legs. Touch your hands to your toes, and let the energy flow down your arms and legs into the ground. Stand, feel the energy come back up, and consider these words of Eckhart Tolle: "When you become conscious of being, what is really happening is that being is becoming conscious of itself".
- Then sit down and write for ten minutes about what this quote means to you.
- Second Writing Exercise: Write for ten minutes about your critics. Tell them everything you can about how they made you feel. Swear if you want to, use exclamation points and words and write in bold capitol letters.
- Third Writing Exercise: Write for ten minutes about how these critics might have helped you. At the end, write "I am grateful to you, critic, for..." and list three items.
- Fourth Writing Exercise: Write for ten minutes about some unexpected highlights and pleasant surprises in your writing so far.
- Fifth Writing Exercise: Look back through your portfolio and

circle some words that hit a nerve ending or imparted a charge as you wrote them. Take a separate sheet of paper and begin a list of these special words.

- By yourself or with your group, refer to the examples of these writing exercises in the Addendum.

CHAPTER SEVEN

"Portraits of You and Your Family"

"Everybody is original if she speaks for herself. So remember these two things: you are talented and you are original. I say this because self-trust is one of the very important things in writing".
Brenda Ueland

The Voice

What might be the most exciting terrain you encounter in this writing is happening now. It is the emergence of your very own voice.

You have witnessed your writing unfold in the previous chapters, and you've come through with flying colors, now aware of your individual preferences, home and natural environments, your body and its senses.

As you have first shown up on the page, and continued to trust that your writer has significant words to say, you have made significant leaps of faith and proved that you can write.

The history of the family is the topsoil that leads to deeper immersion, and as you take off one layer at a time through this writing process, the stories of your family are the source of much significant material.

Those of you who have been involved in music or the performing arts know it is common knowledge that you have a unique voice to train. So it is with writing: Your voice has a unique vibration, richness and tone.

When I understood this was after meeting in a writers' group in Venice, California that convened over ten years every Thursday night. It became clear than whenever one of the group decided to read her work, it was as if an equally recognizable voice of the writer spoke as well. And years later, even when we had not seen or heard each other read for a long time, this inimitable voice would immediately reappear.

Having witnessed this phenomenon repeated again and again in groups, I can testify to this unique power of all our voices. I saw it as eyes lit up in those first years at the Yellowstone residencies when people first recognized theirs and after these sixteen years of this process, they still do".

"A story is like water that you heat for your bath. It takes messages between the fire and your skin. It lets them meet, and it cleans you"
Rumi

To begin, choose a special family member to describe, preferably from childhood, and indicate why this person is so significant in your life.

Set the timer for ten minutes, and writing faster than you can think, remember when this person accomplished something that surprised you or that you admired, that might have been unexpected. Was it grace under pressure? A funny antic or an answer to a challenge?

Start to embellish how they looked, the clothing they wore, the gait they used as they stepped. What ages were you both and where did you live? Did this action permanently change you, the dynamics between you as parent-child, sibling-sibling? How did it alter the rest of the family dynamics?

Now, time to read this out loud. This might be when you involve a family member, and ask them to tell you what they like about your story. Can they register any new development in the style of your writing?

To understand the greater tides that washed over the family's history, from the smallest details to the larger dynamics, try the next two exercises.

First, think of another family member's pair of shoes and write about what they looked like, and anything about them you can recall. What did their size, color, or shape symbolize to you? How did they walk in them and can you still see them now? What do these shoes mean to you?

"Black leather shoes, men's size 9 solid and sensible. Specially cleaned on a Saturday night for church on a Sunday morning. The sharp smell of polish being pushed into leather with a small brush and then swished to shine with a larger softer brush".

With these words Maggie Stewart, one of the Sophia writing group from Glastonbury, begins a description from her childhood in Ireland. Her vivid words show how these exercises can take off in many directions, all of them with the capacity to evoke illustrious images. Yours will too. Look for the rest of her piece in the Addendum, but not before you embark on your own writing. Trust that whatever you do will indeed be as rich as the others', and theirs as rich as yours.

After you read this exercise out loud to the others, and they read to you, in the next ten minutes, please write about the family from a larger overview perspective. This contrast of the smaller details and larger implications of the portraits of your family will demonstrate how you can stretch the clay of your writing.

What incident changed the story of your immediate family, or pre-arranged your future? You might not have realized it for years after. Is it about ancestors who left a country for another and the bravery they demonstrated? How did these changes eventually affect you?

Felicity Dalton, another Sophia, writes:
"My first twelve years were spent in the home of my Chinese maternal grandparents on the outskirts of Kuala Lumpur, the

capitol of Malaysia. Amber evenings gave way to sultry tropical nights, often pierced by thunderclaps and torrential rain. The evening of May 13, 1969, stands out in my memory. Earlier on, imams sang their dawn prayers from neighborhood mosques and devotees at Indian temples jingled and clanged their way through the day. Hushed conversations revealed there was danger afoot. They'll be coming over the hills with their parangs (scythes)".

The full text of Felicity's piece appears in the Addendum. You will never know what will come up until you try, and that is the power and beauty of this writing! But, rest assured, the indelible trappings of character, your own and those of your chosen subjects, are beginning to see the light of day.

These exercises, if you are doing them in a group, may take over a week to do to appreciate their full measure. All are truly, uniquely your own. Again, remember to do your own before reading the continuation of Maggie's and Felicity's pieces. These two pieces were both done as writing faster than you can think exercises.

List of Exercises

- First Writing Exercise: Write for ten minutes about a special family member, preferably from childhood, and indicate why this person is so significant in your life. Did this person accomplish something that surprised you? Describe how they looked, the clothing they wore, the way they walked. What ages were you both and where did you live? Did this action permanently change you? Did it change our family's dynamics? If so, how?
- Second Writing Exercise: Write for ten minutes about another family member's pair of shoes. What did their size, color, or shape symbolize to you? How did they walk in them? What do these shoes mean to you?
- Third Writing Exercise: Write for ten minutes about an

incident that changed the story of your immediate family, or pre-arranged your future. How did these changes eventually affect you?

• By yourself or with your group, refer to the examples of these writing exercises in the Addendum.

CHAPTER EIGHT

"If the Walls Had Ears"

"It is never too late to be what you might have been"
George Eliot, AKA Mary Ann Evans, 1819-1880

As we look at the writing once again like the headlights of a car where you can "only see as far as the light shines" (from the EL Doctorow quote in Chapter One), this chapter features one of the most popular writing exercises because just by shining the smallest bit of light on this subject, you get so much in return. Remember, "It is never too late to be what you might have been", and doing these writing exercises gives you the opportunity to reveal your history to yourself, and to potentially address what you might have been.

Some stories are personal and linked to happy or difficult times in our families, and others are historical. Still others come from the time that you have lived in history and witnessed memorable events together with your generation. Many also come from our travels back in time through reading books or studying history in school.

Let's start with your childhood. What did those walls hear of your family story, of your forebears or you? Were they happy times or tales of a confusing reality? Write for ten minutes about anything that jumps into your mind. If you want, this is an opportunity to use dialogue in your writing, for a change. Please pick up your pen now and write this question: "Walls from childhood or adulthood, what secrets do you still hold"? In reply, start with a voice that will answer in quotation marks, "I see" or "I hear". What do these walls want to say? What mysteries do they hold? Remember the size of the walls. Were they thick or thin?

"Walls with ears hear stories told to no one else. They are very discreet, those walls. They never betray the secrets and the sighs, the compromises and the lies. What happens if the walls should be worn down or torn apart someday? Do the stories drift off in the air, to be retold in distant places, in other tongues"?

Pauline Royce, Glastonbury

As you finish this exercise and read it aloud to each other, what do you feel you have learned about how your writing can describe detail? Can you see a style emerging yet? Now please start this time with the colors of the walls as you remember another family story. Were they bright yellow? Bland green? A white that was clear and spacious? Or off-white? What do these colors symbolize to you and do you have any additional insights? Write for ten minutes, faster than you can think, about this. Are you beginning to see how your writing can blend with the material of your own unique life?

For another example about how writing can merge with your life and bring about remarkable results, here is a description from Gale Cohen, a Los Angeles writer upon her return to Brooklyn:

"Almost every year I make my way back to Brooklyn, and try to immerse myself in the childhood that obscured the boundaries between my being and stone tenements crushed together shoulder to shoulder: the broad parkways lined with huge old maple trees and wooden benches, alleys hung with clean laundry populated with skinny cats, and hallways witness to secret tears, kisses, and first embraces. My existence blended with the sound of traffic on the avenues, and neighbors talking on a hot summer night, the sharp crack of a Spaulding ball on a broomstick bat early Sunday mornings".

Gale Cohen, Brooklyn

After ten minutes of writing, please put down your pens and read to each other. This is the time to move around, get a drink of water, some fresh air before we continue.

Now please go back to the first writing exercise and identify, if the walls had ears, who they would choose of one or two family members who figured prominently in your life drama. Write about them now for ten minutes, starting with any descriptive details about their height, hair and eye color, and what the walls would say. Then read aloud to one another, and afterwards take another short break.

Ready to begin again? This is the time to write about what impacted your whole generation. For instance, if you were taken with the Civil War in the US, have you ever walked down an old road in the South through the woods and heard the voices from the Civil War? What do their stories have to tell you? Or what about a major world event that occurred as you grew up? The civil rights marches during the 1960s or the large marches to protest the war in Vietnam? The man walking on the moon? The Challenger spacecraft being launched? Hula hoops and space wand crazes?

Or in Glastonbury, one senses the time of the dissolution of the abbeys by Henry VIII in 1538. And in England, there are still reverberations from the Battle of Hastings in 1066 when William the Conqueror arrived from France. What historical 'walls that have ears' are you most intrigued by? For ten more minutes, think of any of the above historical incidents that moved you, or any similar historical event. Proceed to write about it. How did you feel about the event, and how did it impact your whole generation?

As in the last chapter, there must now be words you want to circle that are charged with nerve endings for your writing. Ask those who are listening to you read what they like most about your writing.

Now, to switch channels rapidly, one way to charge up your

writing, name three little secrets from your own personal walls that have ears. Set the timer and then write faster than you can think. Allow the writing to stretch a bit further, like clay. Pretend there are clues that wait for you in your writing, and watch what comes easily to you when you least expect it.

This is the last chapter in the section of the book on The Individual, a fitting completion to the writing that has clarified information about you and your status as an individual on the globe. Now we will take up topics that deal more with the collective voice. If at any time you want to go back and do any of the exercises again in the previous chapters, they will always bring new insights and energy to your writing.

The material called forth from the walls of your life has a condensed quality, like packed earth. The more you do this exercise, more will be revealed. Continue to go back over these exercises and bring up new characters from your family or past.

Like a mountain stream that begins in one place and works its way steadily, drop by drop, until the rock falls away and the path of the water is made clear, your words will forge their own indomitable path. The material from these last two chapters always help to give it structure.

List of Exercises

- First Writing Exercise: Write about anything that comes to your mind for ten minutes about what walls with ears still hold of your family stories. If you want, use dialogue in your writing and begin by writing the question, "Walls from childhood or adulthood, what secrets do you still hold?" In reply, start with a voice that answers in quotation marks, "I see" or "I hear". Physically describe the walls; were they vertical or horizontal, think or thin?
- Second Writing Exercise: This exercise is to be done again, and this time please start with the colors of the walls that will

hopefully reveal more details of your family stories.

- Third Writing Exercise: Go back to the first writing exercise and identify, if the walls had ears, who would they choose of one or two family members who figured prominently in your life drama? Write about them now for ten minutes, starting with any descriptive details about their height, hair and eye color, and what the walls would say.
- Fourth Writing Exercise: Write for ten minutes about a historical event or incident that impacted your whole generation, and how you felt about it.
- Fifth Writing Exercise: Make a list of three items: "What are three secrets you haven't shared with anyone"? Remember, they can be light or serious. Then write for ten minutes about one secret you have never shared before.
- By yourself or with your group, refer to the examples of these writing exercises in the Appendix.

~

Section 3
Writing for the Higher Self

~

CHAPTER NINE

"What Would You Like Future Generations To Know One Hundred Years From Now?"

"The future belongs to those who believe in the beauty of
their dreams"
Eleanor Roosevelt

Our children are the future that we will never know. This is a moment when you can use the tool of your writing to record your highest aspirations for what lays beyond your personal horizons while the potential impact of your prose goes much further.

We have examined the voice and other aspects of writing in previous chapters, and now the next important element to address is The Audience". Who are you writing for? The exercises in this chapter allow you to experiment with this new question. As seen in the last chapter "If the Walls Had Ears" has been a favorite among the groups, this exercise "What Would You Like Future Generations To Know One Hundred Years From Now"? is definitely another.

The previous chapter offers us the opportunity to look back and come to terms with some of our family history. This chapter gives you the prowess to look forward and fulfill any desires you might have in creating your own special legacy.

What, through the years, have you fantasized about that you would like to leave behind? Take the rudder now. Look to the compass to use it to your best advantage for your intentions towards the future.

There are many versions on this quote "The future belongs to those who believe in the beauty of their dreams" and one card, that says "the future belongs to those who believe in the *future* of their dreams" has the picture of a boy in a Buster Brown outfit, as if from the 1930s, who has a biplane in his hand he raises to the sky. It is a symbol of hopeful innocence, the young boy, his plane, the arm that reaches to the sky. This creates the tone for how we want to approach the writing in this chapter.

"You were made to give voice to this, your utter astonishment", Annie Dillard, a well-known author spoke in her illustrious *The Writing Life*. With this in mind, now on a much broader plain of writing than we have been before, it is useful to first think of who your audience is again, and jot down a few names or types of people you'd like to write for. Then, think back one hundred years. Who in your family's history was important then, and what were significant moments and events in their lives?

"I think of old newspapers, black print on a broadsheet of old yellowed paper", Stacey Camfield pens in "1908". "No pictures to supplant a thousand words, and I wonder what today's headline might have been all those years ago. My thoughts turn to my relatives passed, folk I never knew, but whose shape and features or mannerisms I might just recognize as a glimmer of something familiar- perhaps in the mirror. Or a hint of history caught in my mother or father's eye. Did they sit and turn the pages of that paper in the morning"?

For instance, less than one hundred years ago, my father experienced the agricultural, industrial and information revolutions in one lifetime. He encountered the Depression of the 1930s in the United States and later assumed responsibility in World War II as a relatively young officer in the Navy. But now that time in history is over, as is his time on this planet. My maternal grandparents came from England exactly one hundred years ago, and I've have often wondered how and what they thought as they encountered this new country, leaving so much tradition behind.

What does this make you think of? By bringing a mere

hundred years of experience into perspective, what do you want to leave behind of the knowledge you have gained?

For your first exercise, go back one hundred years and in the same way that I chose my father and grandparents, write about "What were my past generations thinking and facing in their lives one hundred years ago?" By realizing what you would have appreciated knowing about their lives, you might then be able to guess what future generations would want to know from you. Please write for ten minutes and read what you have written aloud to your writing colleagues.

Now, for a moment's breather, what do you now think of the continued growth of your writing style and its content?

Then try this second exercise that is in two parts. "What have you realized you would like to know from past generations who lived one hundred years ago?"

From this new awareness, what wisdom would you ideally like others to understand one hundred years from now?" As you write, focus on who your audience is. Are they your daughters or sons? Grandchildren? Nieces or nephews? Or a stranger who would walk down the street one hundred years from now?

One idea is to describe how the world of technology looks like now, based on the changes in this last century.

There are many directions you can take. If it's useful to make a list of the kinds of changes you've witnessed first, and then take one item from the list at a time to write about, do so.

Now, for ten minutes, give yourself the license to be like the genie in Aladdin's lamp. You have the world and your posterity at your fingertips! Rub it a little. What figures and fantastic creatures of thought come to the surface?

After writing for these ten minutes, please read your work to each other. Does it sound different from the last chapters? Make notes of the differences. You have this special opportunity right now to be one of history's recorders, especially about this, our completely unique time in history. What of that information should be transmitted to the future?

It's like seeing into the inside of a giant tree that has been cut open with its rings recording what happened from the core to the outermost layer. Writing, in that same way, can captures history, and bring forward from the past the relevance of the present. Then you too can be one whose prophecy is to bear fruit with the words: "the future belongs to those who believe in the beauty of their dreams".

List of Exercises

- First Writing Exercise: First think about who you are writing for. Then, think back one hundred years. Who in your life was important then, and what were significant moments and events in their lives? What were they thinking and facing? Write about this for ten minutes.
- Second Writing Exercise: Write for ten minutes about what you have realized you would like to know from past generations who lived one hundred years ago. Then write about what wisdom you would ideally like others to have one hundred years from now.
- By yourself or with your group, refer to the examples of these writing exercises in the Addendum.

CHAPTER TEN

Celtic Writing Today: Glastonbury's Higher Self

"The Irish Bridge"
"The tiny bridge over a stream is turned by the curve of the road
so that the stone walls stand, not parallel to each other, but
angled; a land only visible when you are not looking; slick shine
touch from ten thousand fingertips have surfaced the top rock
into smoothness now; like water, or curve of overhanging tree,
this bridge once had a given name from a time when people had
a true relationship with the small places and named them in
keeping with their essence..."
Maggie Stewart, Glastonbury

A highlight of my time in Glastonbury has been sharing the women writers' connection to the ancient and contemporary landscape. The passage of generations and much else has emerged from our sharing together.

I have always been entranced by the legends and mysteries of England. The milestones of my grandparents' arrival to the States from Yorkshire, what I felt when I opened my first copy of the Celtic Tree Oracle book and card deck, and most significantly, when I encountered the extraordinary stone in Avebury, England's largest stone circle, in 1985 (subject of the manuscript *Awakening in Avebury: A Woman's Call to Pilgrimage*).

Many a night the Sophia group wrote with inspiration near the Blue Lyas stone hearth composed of the same stones as the ones at Stonehenge. In this centuries-old home on Chilkwell Street, where underneath the floor coursed the Red and White

Springs of the famous Chalice Well, the writings embraced the unique flavor of the ever-present green of Celtic mythology imbued with ancient truths from the lands of the west. As we watched the pale light of Imbolc together, rejoiced in the bursting forth of Beltaine in the spring, or succumbed to the deeper fires of Samhain in late fall, we marked the days of the Celtic calendar and transformed these sacred rites of passage into contemporary writing.

"Our lives
spiraling inwards
downwards
from the dizzy heights of summer;
The black hem of Samhain's skirt
just visible,
swirling at the edge
of the spiral
as I follow
the deadening race downwards
inwards;
Taking me back
into my seeding ground
to meetings along the way
with the grandmothers
of the seed
from which I came,
who wove a shawl of blood around me,
warm, dark, comforting;
From "About Samhain" by Ingelise Jensen, Glastonbury

For your enjoyment, you can read the entire writings by Maggie and Ingelise, in the Addendum of this book.

"Listen to the music within your soul
While listening, do you not feel
An inner self awakening deep within you
That is by its strength that your head is lifted,
That your arms are raised,
That you are walking slowly towards the light?"
Isadora Duncan

Now, for your first writing exercise, take the CD (that was mentioned in the "What You Will Need" section before the first chapter) and put it on your CD player. If you would like to stay in this same theme of the Celtic mysteries, find a CD by Loreena McKennitt who is a favorite. Her "Book of Secrets" is especially evocative of the Celtic world.

If you are drawn by another culture, perhaps the one in which you grew up, please put on a CD from that world. World music, from Mexican, Brazilian, African, Hawaiian and European, is becoming more dynamic every day. Choose one in the group that you can agree upon. There will be time later to play others together, or in your own sanctuary for your own meditation and writing.

The main objective is to clear all space to listen. Play a song, and then play it again. Let it course through your body. Then, when you are ready, please pick up your pen, and write about "What are the ancient images that come from this music to me?" As you repeat Isadora Duncan's words, "Listen to the music within your soul", what myths or legends suddenly spring to mind that you might have heard from early in your childhood or from your parents or grandparents? What stories still dwell somewhere far back in your memory of your ancestral mythic past?

Daphne Garland wrote after to listening to the music:

"The abbey all alone in the vastness of the hills, the heather clad hills, reflecting in the water of the lake. Hear how the sound goes over the lake, it leaves not a ripple ñ the ripples are just made by the fish, the waterboatmen, the moorhens, coots and ducks but the sound slides over unnoticed by the water. The smell in the air of the boggy peat land around the lake mingles with the heather, no breeze, no air, just stillness and upon this stillness the pure sweet voice of youth raised in praise, song and the joy of the moment".

While these words from or about this ancient homeland move me, there must be connections to other lands as memorable to you. "What calls to you over a distant past landscape? What are the words that they want to say"? Try this ten-minute exercise. If you need a jump-start to your writing, go back to any of the above-excerpted poems, re-read them, and write what quickly comes to mind.

For your next exercise in this chapter, let's try to stretch the imagination of your writing by crafting a fictional story. Allow any imagery from a long time ago, possibly drawn from films, books, or family legends to come forward. I'll work along side you and write about mystery ships with pirates, with fogs and long mists over water. You have much at your disposal. Write for ten minutes and share.

From my entry while leading a sacred site tour to Cornwall:

"Green, green. Lush. Water so silent, trickling drop by drop in the deep well, a silence like a deep roar in the reclaiming stillness".

Perhaps this was one of the landscapes poet John O'Donohue could have been describing when he wrote the following in *Anam Cara*: "The Celts had an intuitive spirituality, informed by mindful reverent attention to landscape. It was an outdoor spirituality impassioned by the erotic charge of the earth".

One way to recharge your writing is to connect with the earth. Think about it: As women, we carry it in a special way within us.

You will relish this next exercise. Go outside to a plot of grass. Take your shoes off and stand in it and feel its presence under your feet, and it prickles your toes. Think of all the other times, from childhood to now, that you've had meaningful encounters just by standing on the earth and taking in all that is around you, all through the senses. Allow this energy to course through your body.

Then, when you return to your writing room, to embellish your writing even further, put on another CD and dance. And finally, after some minutes, take out your pen again and write about anything that comes up for you at this time, especially what you felt when you connected to the ground below your feet. I promise you and your writing will be energized. (In fact, at any other time that you feel tired or when the words don't seem to be flowing as effortlessly as you would like, go back outside and do this exercise over again).

Glastonbury, a center for this contemporary Celtic pulse of the earth and its environs are poetically described here by two of the Sophias:

An excerpt from "A Place Where I Have Been That Is Calling Me" by Maggie Stewart:

"Today I walked out on the levels ñ high dry grasses flagging their shaggy tops in unison; I drew my shawl closely around me and knew I had walked this way before. Reaching for the brittle shells of broken reed stalk, I felt in the memory of my fingers the sinew of course reed thread stripped for weaving".

and from "The Spiral Path" by Ingelise Jensen:
"As my hesitant feet
Seek out the steps
Hidden in the moonless dark,

The trace of that Ancient Path
Faintly starts taking form;
Slowly it fills all around me
In space
In ground
And within me
The wet leafy smells fill my nose
The dankness swelling my eyes,
Here choice is not an option
As it was then
In that far-away time
Before my eyes had learnt
To see the world from within,
To know
The inner side of the world
And the vastness of Her realm.
Her presence is strong, unmistakable
Old Mother of the Deep
The power of Her Place
Is immediate
The potent stillness
Shrinking,
The veil of the Worlds".

List of Exercises

- First Writing Exercise: From a CD that has special meaning to you from a personal or cultural point of view, play a song, and then play it again. Then pick up your pen and write about "What are the ancient images that come from this music to me? What myths or legends come to mind that you might have heard from early in your childhood or from your parents or grandparents? What stories still dwell somewhere far back in your memory?
- Second Writing Exercise: What ancient connections are

memorable to you? What calls to you over a distant past landscape? What are the words that they say? Write for ten minutes about this.

- Third Writing Exercise: Stretch your writing by fictionalizing it. Allow any imagery that comes from this past, fueled by films or books that you would like to play with. What about pirates or mystery ships, fogs and mists over long peninsulas near the sea? Remember King Arthur, the Grail myths, the Mists of Avalon! Allow the unexpected to come up.

- Fourth Writing Exercise: To charge your writing, take your shoes off and stand in a patch of grass. Come back in, put on Another CD, and dance. Write about anything that comes up at all. You'll be pleasantly surprised.

- By yourself or with your group, refer to the examples of these writing exercises in the Addendum.

CHAPTER ELEVEN

"The Collective World Voice"

"I've been to Hollywood, I've been to Redwood,
I've been a miner for a heart of gold"
From a song by Neil Young

Writing, in its greatest capacity, has the huge potential for us to dive into the seas of our individuality where we bring up the bright, glistening fish of our being.

The fistfuls of baubles from our subconscious always surprise and even flatter us, as so many of these jewels had never been brought up to the surface before.

But, since we are at our most intrinsic, part of a larger collective whole, our connection to this global consciousness is as much our "heart of gold" as the smaller, more compartmentalized units that we have been mining.

This chapter has been designed to be at the end of the book, since we have now gone deep into the well of our beings through this process, and have re-emerged with not only heightened awareness of our writing abilities, but of ourselves.

Please take a piece of paper, and write what first comes to mind when you hear, "What are three global issues you are most concerned about?" Global warming, the state of the waters, overpopulation would be the first on my list. Then there is education, health care, efforts for world peace, food on the planet and the list goes on. These are large topics, and this list will help you carve a perspective to address them. Pen in hand, warrior that you are, strike away at one of these issues!

Write about what most concerns you in regards to the first item on your list. What do you think should be done about it, and what would be the first step to make some identifiable change? After you go for ten minutes, and share your contribution with the others, be aware that many pieces that have been composed in these workshops and retreats have been accepted as articles or for editorial columns in local or national newspapers and magazines. Consider that your piece could appear in one of these periodicals, and make a difference!

This is one of the first proving grounds for using your writing to enhance the quality of life for you and those around you as well as your community. Many a workshop participant has heard the rallying phrase from me: *"The world needs your words"*.

"I ended up at a creative writing group this weekend; But the material didn't feel as if it wanted to remain with the individual who had written it or even stay in the province of a select few. It was as if the words were clamouring to reach the whole world mind".

Jackie Crovetto, Glastonbury

For exercise two, take up your pens again, and start to write to: "Is there a civic issue you've always had an opinion about, but never voice"? Now is the time to do it. Please write for ten minutes on this thought-provoking theme and then share your results with each other.

"Consciousness Raising" was a term used for elevating women's consciousness about the important roles and abilities they could contribute to society in the 1960s and 1970s. As we now write in the new global consciousness, and are bolstered by progress achieved years ago, it is clear we become closer through the universal themes that emerge when we share our writing.

In Glastonbury, the groups of women are from England, Ireland, Denmark, Sweden, Australia and the United States, and their mixture of voices includes material also experienced in Africa, India, and the Middle East. Even though these stories have taken place in different parts of the globe, there is a remarkable resemblance in their content. Sharing personal, familial, romantic and political themes in this moving and universal way, it is clear that the thread of connection among women writers grows bigger everyday.

In the book *Who Dies?* Death and Dying pioneer Stephen Levine mentions that 200,000 people leave our earth sphere every day. (The book was published in the 1980s, so this number must be much higher today.) In the eye-blink of a moment we are on this planet. Take a moment to consider what this means to you and your writing.

For the next writing exercise, plunge into: "What conditions do you feel must be urgently addressed right now"? Please write for ten more minutes and share your pieces together.

As vibrant as we are as individuals, this radiance only increases as we recognize we are part of a collective world voice that gets stronger as more of us become aware of it.

Now, for your last exercise, take on: "The life I cannot not live, the writing I cannot not write". You will encounter some surprises, for there is an invincibility in your writing that exists here.

Remember, when one of us moves forward, we all move forward!

NOW WELCOME YOUR VOI CE TO THE COLLECTIVE WORLD WHOLE.

List of Exercises
- First Writing Exercise: List three global issues that concern you. Then pick one and write for ten minutes about it. What do you think should be done about it, and what would be the first step to make some identifiable change?

- Second Writing Exercise: Is there a civic issue you've always had an opinion about, but never voiced? Now is the time. Write for ten minutes about this.
- Third Writing Exercise: Write for ten minutes about the global conditions that you feel must be urgently addressed right now.
- Fourth Writing Exercise: Write for ten minutes about "The life I cannot not live, the writing I cannot not write".
- By yourself or with your group, refer to the examples of these writing exercises in the Addendum.

CHAPTER TWELVE

From Isolation to Universal Sharing:
The Divine Feminine Circle

"Life is standing at the edge of an abyss of forgetfulness waiting
for the light of the world to be born. This birth needs the
wisdom of the feminine, and for women to take their place in
this time of great potential".
Llewellyn Vaughn-Lee, *The Call and the Echo*

On my morning walk past Sunset Beach towards Pipeline, where
some of the world's major surfing contests are held on the north
shore of Oahu, Hawaii, I move under towering tropical vines,
brash colors and giant flowers, bright red fuchsias to wild purple
orchids. Exotic fruits and gourds lay at my feet.

Suddenly I am stopped by an intense image. I have a stetho-
scope in my hand and am holding it against a huge female belly.
I am being asked to "listen, listen" to what the soon-to-be-born
being within is saying. It is way larger than any normal female's,
like the giant ballooning belly of a woman of color mother earth,
the Divine Feminine.

Part of the strength of this writing process is that it literally
brings women to sit together in circles that author Jean Shinoda
Bolen has epitomized in her book *The Millionth Circle*. It's where
we hear our universal truths.

When the first inklings of this book came after teaching this
specialized writing process for years, its compelling thrust was to
cut through the isolation that so many feel in this world. The
McDonaldized society that surrounds us with all its brand new
technological toys implies that there should be no reason to feel
alone, but in contrast, it can make the isolation even stronger.

Since starting to write the first chapter, what has pulled me forward has been another image of a woman, one who perpetually sits by her radio in some remote village or town, who waits to hear the women's groups read their writing on the radio. I could almost see the clothes she wore as she waited intently, knowing that these words were essential to her life, that they would create a breakthrough in some way in her consciousness. Radio in the earlier days was important not only for the words that came through it, but for its connection through sound. I've always seen women from the groups reading their remarkable writing on the radio in the future, and I hope someday I'll meet this woman and be able to thank her for giving me the motivation to continue to write this book.

"For human culture to change, for there to be "the hundredth monkey, for patriarchy to become balanced by the discerning wisdom and compassion that are associated with the feminine aspects of humanity, there has to be the millionth circle. That is because what the world needs now is an infusion of the kind of wisdom women have and the form of that circle itself is an embodiment of that wisdom".

Jean Shinoda Bolen

"What are you wearing today?" As the heartbeat of this newly emerging Divine Feminine being pulses near all of us, look down at your attire. How did you choose to express yourself through the colors, the contours of the clothing, the shoes? Pick up your pen and start to write, faster than you can think, about what they personify about the inner you, your essence? Then, in the same exercise, what else is there to recognize about yourself today, and how you chose to come here to the pages of your writing?

"We are all here on temporary feet, says Stephen Levine, in his book *One Year To Live*. For your next exercise, write about "What is it that your 'temporary feet' most want to do? Do they want to dance, to climb a mountain, to swim in the ocean"?

As you carry this torch of Divine Feminine wisdom into society, as you listen to your heartbeat and the larger one of this new consciousness, think about the 'temporary feet'
in the context of your life in the next ten minutes of writing.

Go back to Chapter Nine ("What I would like to write for people to hear one hundred years from now?"), and using the filter of that far-reaching visualization, please think again about this paragraph from the beginning of the book:

"One woman spoke at the beginning of the day (in a 'Writing for the Higher Self' workshop) feeling desolate at the world situation as important to effect any change on a world scale yet after writing one piece she said she had this inexplicable sense that something had changed, and that it felt as if somehow that had influenced the whole, changed something in a subtle but radical way". Jackie Crovetto, Glastonbury

To employ the energy you have brought out in the last two exercises, and for the purposes of voicing your own divine wisdom at this time, "What change would you like to effect with your voice today"?

Take a moment to breathe and get a glass of water. If need be, walk around before you plunge in. Then remember your heartbeat, the larger heartbeat, and begin to write for ten minutes. Anything you say or do is perfect.

At the end of ten minutes, share the words with your allies. How do you and they feel?

Now, to review, how has it been to watch your voice emerge? Please note its evolution and development over these past weeks. Has more than one voice emerged? If so, how would you distinguish what it is like? (Anything you say here is perfect).

You've been on your own pilgrimage during this course to the further depths and reaches of your writing. And, simultaneously, you've created a circle with other aspiring women. How do you want this circle to continue? After writing for ten minutes about the development of your voice (above), reading and sharing with the others, now please set the timer and write about the outcome from this next question:

How do you visualize this circle being the foundation for more inspired work together? It is as important to speak about this with each other as to write about it, but do write about it as well for the next ten-minute exercise.

During moments in the library of the Glastonbury Abbey Retreat House when the group read from the writing of the day, I'd look up at the ceiling and sense there were invisible choruses of women who had written in the past. "Go on! Go on! The world needs your voice now. Do it for all of us"! they seemed to say.

Let your writer hear intuitively what first comes from these cheers. What is your answer to these honorary voices propelling us on?

"Sophia is the goddess of our time", celebrated Celtic author Caitlin Matthews has written,. "By discovering her we will discover ourselves and our real response to the idea of a Divine Feminine principle. When that idea is triggered in common consciousness, we will begin to see the upsurge in creative spirituality".

Whether they were the Sophias of the Glastonbury Abbey choruses, the contemporary Sophias and other excelling women writers of Glastonbury, or women writers everywhere who are emerging to find their voices and make them known, this creative spirituality is alive and well!

List of Exercises

- First Writing Exercise: Write for ten minutes about what you are wearing today. How did you choose to express yourself through the colors, the contours of the clothing, the shoes?

What do they personify about the inner you, your essence? Then, in the same exercise, what else is there to recognize about yourself today, and how you chose to come here to the pages of your writing?

- Second Writing Exercise: "We are all here on temporary feet". says Stephen Levine, death and dying visionary, in his *One Year To Live*. Write for ten minutes about what your "temporary feet' most want to do. Do they want to dance, to climb a mountain, to swim in the ocean?

- Third Writing Exercise: Refer to Chapter Nine. Then, to employ the energy you have brought out in the first two exercises, and for the purposes of voicing your own divine wisdom at this time, write for ten minutes about what change would you like to effect with your voice today.

- Fourth Writing Exercise: Write for ten minutes about the development of your voice. How has it been to watch your voice emerge? Note its evolution and development over the past weeks. Has more than one voice emerged? If so, how would you distinguish what it is like?

- Fifth Writing Exercise: Write for ten minutes about how you visualize your circle being the foundation for more inspired work together.

- Sixth Writing Exercise: Listen to the invisible chorus of women who have written in the past. What emerges from these cheers? What is your answer to these honorary voices propelling us on?

- By yourself or with your group, refer to the examples of these writing exercises in the Addendum.

CHAPTER THIRTEEN

Bringing the Soul Back Home: Writing Exercises for the Higher Self

"I believe real art, in whatever form it takes, is our essence
revealed and expressed. And to me, this act of courageously
offering your essence can benefit the world and be a wonderful
act of love"
Ann O"Shaunessey, *Soul Flares*

What has given me the conviction to write this book is that, throughout the years of this teaching, I have worked with so many people who hope their efforts will benefit the common good. And they wish in particular that their writing will touch someone who needs inspiration or is moved to transformation.

These writing exercises for the higher self carve out one's stellar abilities at writing while underscoring the direction that Thomas Moore brought to popular attention in *Care of the Soul: A Guide for Cultivating Depth and Sacredness in Everyday Life.*

The soul steers us to the greatest heights of self-recognition, and these exercises are designed to be a mirror for that process. Now, as the most recent graduates of writing in the new consciousness, when you review what you've done in these last weeks, do you see the range of style, voice, and rhythm you've accomplished for your portfolio?

It is time to take hold of your Golden Chalice as a symbol of the lasting results you've gained from these exercises, and imagine it before you. What are your first feelings about it? As you may have noticed, this writing technique allows you to go both deeper into the layers of your individual self and your families' histories while scanning the horizon of the future. Using this radiating light, as far as the headlights can shine in both directions, this is your moment of golden expression.

Pick up your pen, set the timer for ten minutes, and as you do, place your imaginary chalice before you. What does it look like? Is it made of crystal or ceramic? Does it stand tall in the foreground or does it still linger behind the veils (remembering the parting of the veils and the ' Mists of Avalon' to bring it through) for you to bring it into the light? When you are through, share this with the others.

"Once the soul awakens, the search begins and you can never go back. From then on, you are inflamed with a special longing which will never again let you linger in the lowlands of complacency and partial fulfillment. The eternal makes you urgent."

From *Anam Cara: Spiritual Wisdom for the Celtic World*, by John O'Donohue

John ODonohue's quote from *Anam Cara* is mentioned again here to set the soulful tone for this new quest of yours to understand what your chalice means to you. He delivered this opus to the world and only a few years later, at age 52, died in his sleep, having given this tremendous gift of lyricism to the world.

For the second exercise, let's ask this Chalice: "How will my relationship to you be of service to the larger humanity"? Then, the third exercise: "How will it be of service to me"? Take your time to think about both questions, then answer this second one in ten minutes with a break in between. (Time to nosh on tea and biccies if you're in the UK, or juice and carrot cake if you're in the US, noodles and green tea if you're in the Far East, or a shot of espresso if you're in Europe.)

These are large impactful questions, so if you would like to separate them and do them in different sessions, that's fine. However, you might find that their symmetry will give you greater insight. Then, return again to the page. Make sure you take plenty of time to read out loud between the exercises, and read a second time as well (that always helps to hear it again, and read slowly and more loudly).

Always remember, you have support from the universe to undertake this writing that will always be with you. Review your material, and the exercises will give you added momentum to pick the writing up again.

I suggest that you purchase an actual chalice to place near you while you write. Mine is a light green shade of jade, and was purchased at the Chalice Well Gift Shop in Glastonbury many years ago. It is relatively small, with a lotus flower at the base of its cup, round like the sun, a circle. I like that it is from Vietnam, a particularly significant place for those living in the United States, especially now that the country is a place of peace.

Do you see your Chalice filled with liquid that bubbles with laughter or is its water so deep you can hardly see the bottom of it? It will appear in many different ways in your time together.

Now, I leave you with one of the biggest challenges you will face in your writing (hey, that's why it's called 'calmly risking writing'!) Since you have risen to the occasion to become part of the "collective world voice" how do you intend to embrace "the other' in your writing?

Standing by the glorious stones in Avebury, England's largest stone circle, I have often thought of the past Neolithic agricultural society that dwelled there in approximately 3500-3300 B.C. One with the earth and its seasons and the endless cycle of the sun and moon, no recorded history or electrical lighting, this matriarchal culture celebrated each year when spring returned as the symbol of the regeneration of nature. In ceremony, in fire circles around the stones, they renewed their promises of commitment to revere the earth and then processed to honor the souls of their community at sacred sites by travelling many miles on foot.

Even though, now, centuries later we are bolstered by the implements of technology, we stand on the earth in the same way. As a human species, our fragility is our strength because it makes us equally dependent on one another, bound by the commonality of our collective brief time on this planet. This is where your writing, if you assume the task, can speak legions.

One of the highlights of the sacred site tours for women writers I've led over the past six years has been our entrance into the inner circle of Stonehenge at sunrise. Driving through the dark from Glastonbury to get there by dawn, we pass by statuesque trees and lumbering animals whose forms become more distinct in the mist as the light grows. Then we reach this monumental plain as the pink of dawn warms the sky and go single file into the ancient mythological site. After our time in the inner sanctuary, we end in a circle to put blessings for dear ones and the world into it.

The words I was moved last time to put in the circle while pouring sacred well water from my Chalice on the ground were: "May we see the 'Other' as ourselves and bring them into our healing here today. May there be only inclusion, not exclusion, and connection, not disconnection with all those who appear to be the 'Other' from different races, tribes, and families than our own".

Now, light a candle and set yourself up for the next exercise: "What blessings would you like to make for connection and inclusion"?

As we now move to the end of this book, how do you see this 'Other' in your life, and how would you like to create a connection to that being, or group of beings? Can you actually see them as parts of yourself? Whether it is a family member, a personal friend, someone you work with, or groups/tribes you have read about in the newspapers, write about how you can climb out of your perceived differences, and bring them into your circle of life.

It has been my pleasure to help you "Bring Your Soul Back Home".

One day you may read your own writing from these chapters on the radio, with us, or you'll hear the writing on the radio. Your portfolio of work may appear in the next book's anthology of women writers' work (*Bringing the Soul Back Home* #2) or you'll present a book of it to your friends, family and community. Think of it creating an even larger ripple in the world! Or, if you prefer, it may be your own quiet testament to yourself that brings you nurturing and fulfillment at the end of the day and is with you, as friend and companion, for many more.

May it heal you from your depths. Take with you these blessings from this last writing from Glastonbury, written from the following direction "I speak so soft that you will only catch mere snatches of phrases, let the spaces between echo your own longing":

"Streams of consciousness
Tapestries of connections
Woven dreams filtering into life,
What does life want to whisper
Out of this place of long unheeded silence"?
Jackie Crovetto, Glastonbury

THIS IS YOUR TIME, WHAT WILL YOU WRITE?
RAISING YOUR GOLDEN CHALICE:

JUST WRITE!!

List of Exercises

- First Writing Exercise: Write for ten minutes about your imaginary chalice. What does it look like? Is it made of crystal or ceramic? Is it filled with liquid that bubbles with laughter or is its water so deep you can hardly see the bottom of it?
- Second Writing Exercise: Ask your chalice: "How will my relationship to you be of service to the larger humanity"?
- Third Writing Exercise: Ask your chalice: "How will my relationship to you be of service to me"?
- Fourth Writing Exercise: Write for ten minutes about blessings that you would like to make for connection and inclusion. How do you see the "other" in your life, and how would you like to create a connection to that being, or group of beings? Can you actually see them as parts of yourself? Write about how you can climb out of your perceived differences, and bring them into your circle of life.
- By yourself or with your group, refer to the examples of these writing exercises in the Addendum.

ADDENDUM

WOMEN'S WRITING FROM THE GROUPS FOR BRINGING THE SOUL BACK HOME: WRITING IN THE NEW CONSCIOUSNESS PLEASE NOTE:

What follows are some examples of Women's Writing from the groups I have worked with. Some pieces are a result of spontaneous writing faster than you can think exercises, while others are more polished. They are here for your enjoyment and encouragement, so remember to keep your critics firmly in their jar! Everyone's writing has its own distinctive voice, passion and unique value as it makes its way into the world, including yours, which we look forward to seeing!

CHAPTER ONE: THE SPONTANEOUS WRITING PROCESS

Spontaneous Writing #1
("Write about something in this room, without stopping")
The fluted bowl in the center of the room looks like it is made of the water it contains. Blue and brown rimmed, it is the shape of a tulip whose petals have joined hands. The cup beside it complements the bowl in color and form. Both are shiny, glossy, heavy, like the wet earth of which they are made.

What bowl is this? What container, symbol of the feminine, like the boxes, those non-existent boxes in my recent dream: the man, keeper of the nourishment, said to me, "No boxes; no food". How cold he was and how cleverly manipulative, like the FEMA of our recent hurricanes.

But we women, we have boxes. That's who we are. That's even the nickname that high school boys of the 1950s called us: Box. It was meant to be demeaning, but in fact, it represents our ability to contain, to hold, to be with, to stay in there through thick and through thin, that distinguishes us women. We are the relationship holders and builders, the mothering ones, the ones who can easily create circles and webs and safety net. While the world goes wackily to and fro, we contain, are the containers, the boxes, the bowls, the vases, the bearers of beauty and of water.

Her water broke, we say, as the baby is coming forth in birth. The water and the waiting. The water, as in we are 98% water. The water of our depths, we former mermaids, nursemaids house-maids. What of the handless maiden; what was her story again? We are made in His/Her Likeness, the androgynous One - the one containing both male and female, compassion and strength. The bowl of water is water, but also contains the water, translucent, transparent, transporting, transmogrifying, transfiguring, trans-lating, trans-Atlantic, like Katya's current life. She is creating the container for us here. If we want it. The nebulousness is its strength, like the bowl and the water. What looks like a bowl is not, and yet is. "That's the beauty of the thing", she said.

MARILYN SEQUOIA, RIVERSIDE, CALIFORNIA

"Writing faster than you can think or about an object in the room":

"The very first piece on the very first night in the darkening Sophia Room in the Glastonbury Experience area followed some talk about creative writing and a direction from Katya that went straight to my heart:

the sacred space of inner light and
the gentleness of self-regard

The few lines I wrote in response came bumbling out, probably from that inner sanctuary which my Grandmother's treasured garden became for me as a child, but in no particular order of sequence.

We called our Grandmother Hamme:

"The Sacred Garden that holds me and allows me to be whatever do what is in me at the moment.

I am regarding myself in the sunlight, helping the hesitant, cautious, unsure youngster slip out; helping her move her feet forward, one by one, revealing the light in her being: Hamme's Garden of treasures where I became the imagined other, overlooked in secret by the creatures living there, fish and plants, the naked boy in bronze standing tall by the gate down to the sea (guarding the gateway between above and below); the other naked boy hiding behind the bushes, peeing water into the flowers".

INGELISE JENSEN, GLASTONBURY

"I choose the dried contorted willow in a vase in the Sophia Room"

"Contortion-this way that way and the other. I am but a branch, once lively, now dead and dried. Had leaves once, to sense and feel and touch the wind.

I lived once and was part of a whole, an entire tree. I remember the swaying in the breeze, the soft gentle rain, the mists coming over me, flowing around, then.

I remember the wind, the howling, roaring wind, tearing leaves and branches from the tree that was my whole, and the torrential rain, beating down, cascading in a waterfall all over me. As part of my whole and being a tree, I remember the roots in the ground, soaking up the water, seeking out nutrients. I remember the air around me, of oxygenation, of sunlight , sometimes hot and very drying, sometimes gentle, but always bright and awakening.

I remember with gladness the use to which my whole has been used for others, the rabbit at my roots, the birds in my hair, landing stages for all who came, all shapes and sizes. Insects took nourishment from me and found safe places to hide, a kaleidoscope of all comers, all callers, all dwellers.

And now I am here, no more a proud part of my whole but just a dried reminder of that which I once was ñ proud and alive and beautiful. And yet I know I am still beautiful, I still have my shape and my form but I no longer feel the breeze on my skin or the touch or rain or the sunlight caressing me, I now collect a little dust, a little attention, so sad to end this way but I know I still give pleasure to those who would look closely at my form. No two twigs are the same but yet I can still hold your attention, all is not lost. I still have my part to play, although small, I am still here. Memories are all that are left to me of how it all was for me. Done and dusted but still a part of the eternal whole, the one whole to which we all belong".

DAPHNE GARLAND, GLASTONBURY

"As I look around the room, the French window takes my attention. Being inside and being able to see outside is so important to me so as not to feel shut in and I am reminded of my thoughts I expressed in the last writing that I had found a link between my inner and outer landscapes. The French window symbolizes that for me".

PAULINE ROYCE, GLASTONBURY

"I am sitting in school. I am little and the room is big and warm, the windows are huge and the sun shines through one to the little round tables where clusters of children paint and play. I am putting coloured pegs into little holes, enjoying the colours and the order and the challenge. I am focused and then my mind is off again, my hearing is acute but selective and the sound of birds draws my mind and my brain right out the window. So I am sitting with my back to the window putting pegs into the holes of the peg board, but I am also (behind) myself out of the window on the grass feeling the sun and hearing the birds, watching and feeling in my other body, the body of my extended self. My black cat Mittens is scrapping with a tiger cat down the road. A part of me is always out of the window with the grass and the animals, where the sky is infinite".

SABRINA DEARBORN, GLASTONBURY

"I wound up at a creative writing group this weekend".

I ended up at a creative writing workshop "Writing for the Higher Self."

Some gems emerged and the people there were talking of an anthology and of some sort of local dramatic presentation for the work. But the material didn't feel as if it wanted to remain with the individual who had written it or even stay in the province of a select few. It was as if the words were clamouring to reach the "whole world mind" and I don't even know exactly what I meant by that!

How to explain this better? One woman spoke at the beginning of the day of feeling desolate at the world situation, as important to effect any change on a world scale. How does one reach the minds of corporate America or politicians? Yet after writing one piece she said that she had this inexplicable sense that something had changed because something within her had softened, opened up, taken a risk and that it felt as if somehow that had influenced the whole, changed something in a subtle but radical way.

On one level it made no rational sense and yet the change was inexplicably tangible and all we had been doing was writing from the heart. That was ALL, putting our whole selves into that one simple activity. It felt very Alchemical and yet so simple and ordinary too".

JACKIE CROVETTO, GLASTONBURY

CHAPTER TWO: WHAT IS YOUR PASSION?
"Why I Write":

"I write to put food on the table, I write because it's dangerous, a bloody risk. I write for alchemy, I write for change. I write because it is an act of faith.

To hold the pen in the hand and write on the page the words that truly matter, that show me the truth of being here, being alive. Being a passionate victim.

The words feel contradictory, but aren't.

My voice is a whimper in the night, but if enough voices cry out, if enough whimpers are heard, if enough fools jump and say "No" then perhaps when we all land, the earth will have moved a quarter inch. That quarter inch would mean the end and the beginning.

I write because I have to or my sanity will crack.

I write because being seven years old, in a small body, coping with adversity, my voice was rarely heard. I write for the children of the world who draw breath, whose pussed sores, malnutritioned bodies and broken legs, I never got to really touch. Whose way of life I gradually became immune to. Whose way of life was touching me all along, but I closed my mind and heart to survive such blistering in my face pain.

I write to clear debt, clear mind and body of suffering. I write for confessions' sake and to say it how it is.

I write to stoke the ardour of passion long since buried, but rekindled and awakened in the pen stroke. I write because my soul demands it of me and because the pen is mightier than the sword and because victims everywhere can raise up their individual burdens and throw them down, victims no longer.

I write because the burning bush told me to. I am the female Moses returned with roughened feet and a wild unconquered heart and I dare to love in the face of disappointments and in the face of desperation, displeasure and ignorance.

I write because it's a dance. I write because of my Dad. My Dad told me to, not in so many words but in a communication beyond time and place.

I write to regain my trust in myself, to find my place, my power and my significance.

I write to extract information and encapsulate communication.

I write because I am brave, foolhardy, humble and resolute.

I write to hear your voice and to let go.

I write to resume duties, but mostly to discover and uncover, to tease out what

really wants to speak. To find the courage to say it as it is.

To transcend weakness by acknowledging it, to transcend strength by using it under weakness' guidance.

I write to obliterate my own lies and giddiness. I write because to do so, relieves me of the burden of truth that sticks in my solar plexus and throat and rarely erupts.

I write to find out what I can write about. Who the artist is. I write because I simply have to, whether heard or alone. I write to make peace with my ancestors and myself.

I write to hear the voice that was squashed speak and marvel at its resonance.

I write simply, simply, simply because I have to".

JACQUELINE REDMOND, GLASTONBURY

"The Writing I can not write. The journey I can not not take"

"The writing I can not not write is the writing that comes from grace. I do not feel what at times appears on the page by the movement of the pen held in the hand that is connected to this body is from me. It seems that some times I simply am called to respond to some flow of feelings that then become thoughts then words on a page. I have only begun writing again after many years. I remember the feeling of that flowing through me and onto a page and I am so grateful when now it comes again. The writing I can not not write comes from grace. The journey I can not not take is that when grace appears I can not not follow her".

VEDA ROUBIDEAUX, IDYLLWILD, CALIFORNIA

"What I feel passionate about":

"The arts, making, creating something, being true, allowing

the living creatures to continue becoming and being themselves.

The making, creating something: the something is important, the outer physical reflection of the inner, felt image.

That image, born in a fleeting now, and gone in the next, maybe held in memory to find the shimmering rainbow bridge into physical creation while I'm finding my courage to let it live and have its own life, out of mine"

INGELISE JENSEN, GLASTONBURY

From the direction, "Dance when you're broken open, when you tear the bandage off, Dance in your blood, then dance when you are perfectly free" (Rumi)

"Dance in the middle of danger, dance when the night is bright, dance when there are no words left, dance when there is no joy. I am unable to articulate. Frozen; feel in the sun wheel. Observer I am, painted on a blue sky...."

JACQUELINE REDMOND, GLASTONBURY

"My Passion"

"I have chosen exercising outdoors, doing projects at home, walking in town or on the trails. Now I need to think about this word passion and how it relates to my choice. Do I feel a passion about exercise and being outside in all kinds of weather among the plants and trees?

I think passion is a feeling held inside that is there before the event. A passion for chocolate, or good coffee happens before that bite or sip. For me walking or working or just spending quiet time outdoors gives me a feeling of inner relaxation that happens only during the event. And if for some time I do not make time for these activities, I do not feel a passion for them but a great discomfort, a kind of longing for something, a feeling of separation from part of my own being. I don't know why this is true for me but over time I have learned it is.

I wonder what else is true for me? Oh! I think I have just

realized what I have a passion for, a feeling held inside the heart of anticipation and great desire.

YES. THIS IS MY PASSION: to truly understand, accept and honor who I am".

VEDA ROUBIDEAUX, IDYLLWILD, CALIFORNIA

CHAPTER THREE
BECOMING PRESENT IN YOUR WRITING: EXPLORING THE BODY AND ITS SENSES

"STRUCTURING"

"My skull,

my skeleton,

my vertebral column.

Seven cervical discs,

twelve thoracic,

five lumbar

five sacral,

and four coccygeal.

My skeletal framework

holds the rest of me together!

It brings me structure

and stability

And protects my vital organs.

I have much to learn

from these wise old bones,

In shaping my writing process".

LORYE KEATS HOPPER, GLASTONBURY

"What is the song I bring?"

"A sound strong and uncompromising

Loud and soft and loud and soft

Sometimes a pattern is discernable and we can call it

a story, a project.

Sometimes it's chaotic, frightening, coming out of the

dark, a wailing, a howl
We call it a poem.
Children in the street playing ball, listening to
their neighbors argue, cry, hollering out
the window 'Dinner is ready, get up here'
This song has a rhythm like footsteps on a staircase
running up five flights of stairs,
Or moving with purpose, and a brave stride, among a
group of young friends, down the
concrete sidewalk.
A song that tells of the colors of the mountains and
valleys. Old homes with fruit trees
in the front yard, and prehistoric looking palm trees,
golden light embracing all.
The song should be brutally honest. Make people who
listen to it uncomfortable. It
should be filled with the tragedies that surround us.
But also the beauty, the great gift of the senses"
GALE COHEN, LOS ANGELES, CALIFORNIA

"Morning at Spirit Mountain Retreat"
It is early morning at Spirit Mountain.
I look up and see that the sky
is a soft dove gray,
the color of dawn that comes
between night and sunrise.
The blue jays are silent
and have not yet found their morning voice.
The air is soothingly soft,
like an emollient.
It bathes me in morning coolness
by a silent, earth hugging breeze
that doesn't stir the leaves on the trees.
There is a fragrant, cool smell to morning dawn.

It is the smell of earth and moist leaf green
not yet made pungent by the heat of the sun.
Now the changing of the dawn
to the beginning of the day comes swiftly
as the sun's rays land on a distant hill.
It has awakened the rat-a-tat-tat
of the wood pecker
and the squawking of the jay bird.
It has awakened the dog
that lives up the hill from Spirit Mountain
as he greets the morning
with prolonged howls.
In a smooth, seamless crawl of sunlight,
like a gentle breaking wave
that sweeps towards a sandy shore,
the nearby oaks and pines are flooded
with a golden hue as the sun
swirls into the ravine next to Spirit Mountain.
I look up and see that the dove gray sky
has burst into a brilliant topaz blue.
It is a blue not seen in the valleys below,
and my day has come alive
with the changing kaleidoscope of colors".
RACHEL DUDEK, RIVERSIDE, CALIFORNIA

CHAPTER FOUR:
NATURE AS THE SPIRIT OF PLACE IN YOUR WRITING

"Untitled"
"I sit in the dirt, nestled by glossy vinca, writing.
I share this page with tiny wandering spiders.
I share this ground with a loose-knit web of writers.
How perfectly satisfying.

I sit at the base of this tree trunk ,
Sinking a taproot from my tailbone.
Like a straw, it draws up from Mother Earth
The dark, rich, sustaining blood of embodiment".
JOAN ZERRIEN, IDYLLWILD, CALIFORNIA

"Spirit of Place in Summer"
"Woods of beech trees
Standing tall, leafy umbrellas
Touching the sky
Suffusing the light
Into gossamer greeny veils
Osmosing through
My protective shell
Greening my being
Embracing my heart,
To dance once more
With the winged ones
Weaving spirals
Through slanted shafts
Of sunlight"
INGELISE JENSEN, GLASTONBURY

"The Rain in LA"
Water rolls over my tongue, teeth and is totally lost in my
belly.
Underground springs in Eagle Rock, coming from the
heart and soul of the San Gabriel Mountains
carry minerals, sandstone flavored by the roots and
fine pollen of the golden and gray chaparral.
The moistened earth that sucks down the precious rain
from bone dry heavens drains through quartz and opal
and clay; the water, traveling up through the fruit trees,
the roses, the endless boxes of backyard faux wilderness,

there in the first bite of the smooth creamy avocados,
the biting lemons, grapefruit and purple grapes.
When the water finally runs down our chins.
The simple glistening connections moving on like time
collecting the history and geography of everything it
touches. Spreading out to spill into the ocean where
it is totally lost".
GALE COHEN, LOS ANGELES, CALIFORNIA
" The Rose is Tearing off her Gown"
(from a Rumi poem)
"The rose is tearing off her gown to show allegiance
to the Sun, unafraid to be bold, she shows the world
and her lover the shape of things to come: pure white
garments gleaming in the sunshine.
Without her efforts where would the rest of the
flowers be? Needing to look for the Rainbow to help
them grow into their own.
Listening to spring grow is like hearing disparate
parts of an orchestra tuning up and crescendo-ing into a
synchronized symphony with no conductor in sight, but
all parts seem to know their entry by heart.
Mother Nature's love is what tweaks those
plantstrings into a tuneful, timely plant performance
of new life. If I stand in the still centre of
silence, I can hear my own grass grow, feeling an
intimate part of Nature's Plan for renewal.
Early daffodils stand shoulder to yellow shoulder,
nodding their gleaming heads in sisterly solidarity,
defying anyone to rob them of their Gold Standard, but
soon to be out-trumpeted by the still peeping tulips,
only just lifting their colours above ground, letting
the sun lick their delicate heads, like the cow gently
licking her calf into life".
INGELISE JENSEN, GLASTONBURY

"Clematis Montana"

"It is in full bloom just outside our front door forming a thick wall of pale pink flowers, densely packed. I have never seen it so lovely. Barry has given it tender loving care throughout the year as last year was a flop. This glorious pink wall fills me with unspeakable delight. The smell transports me into a state of bliss as it enters my nose and then spreads to my whole inside. Everyday I enjoy the sight and balmy smell. Visitors comment on the loveliness. I cannot ever remember having been in love with a plant but my love is fragile. Already some of the blooms are starting to fall off, petals covering the ground underneath. I search for the remaining buds and try to calculate how many more days of clematis bliss remain.

Here we go again, the sadness of the transience of life and the need and greed to hang on to it, wanting it to last forever. And yet, if I am alive next year, I will hopefully be able to enjoy the bliss again.

It is different with us humans. My spring bloom is well past and the fragrance and appeal that comes with it. It just takes a few glances in an old photo album to confirm what time does to the face.

Never again will I enjoy that extraordinary look of desire, delight or even lecherousness from the men who crossed my path.

Here we go again, nostalgia and regret. They do say that after forty a woman is responsible for her looks because it nearly all comes from the inside!

Enjoy and live to the full every day as if it was your last regrets are futile. That is what I keep telling one of my moaning Minnie friends when she goes on and on about a long since lost and hopeless love.

Back to my love, the Clematis Montana. It is enough that I know that it will come back next spring and in the meantime, I can carry the image of its loveliness in my heart.

Life is for living every moment whatever the state of your bloom".

ELISABETH THAM, GLASTONBURY

"What Winter Said to Spring and What Spring Said to Winter"

"My Dearest Spring,

Before I return home I thought it best to pause and make contact. As you know I have been in charge these past few months and my clarity and darkness have been

the predominate tone in recent times.

Let me remind you in brief of the crystalline shapes that dance through the winter nights and take shape from time to time in frost and snow and ice. Let me tell you that these little beauties, like neutrinos, exist in all forms of life. Though the bare bones of harmony and form are most apparent in winter, thy serve as structures and forms upon all of life hangs.

I would caution you to remember this geometric union that we all share lest you fall into the illusion and the attachment to form in and of itself. Form is not

the entire point of creation.

Proceed then in your duties with a balance of memories of the past and enthusiasm for your future.

Remember your essence and enjoy your form. May life continue to be a non-stop ritual and celebration of usefulness.

Love, Winter;

Dear Winter,

Thank you for your memo! It is just like you to go all somber on me just before you leave. Feeling all nostalgic, are we? You come in every year like a thick, black cloak infilling and enfolding us. .I appreciate your care and concern and your sincere desire to se us all held in balance throughout the year. But it's time for the stabilizers to come off and for me to ride out on my own.

I so enjoy this annual crossing over, ships passing and all that.

Yet, I am restless to get on with things. I've got pansies and primulas popping out all over and some fab grape hyacinths that are really hot to trot. The truth is I do know to let them open in little bursts and check in daily with the weather. I'll always remember that particularly warm February where we burst into life all at once and most of us disappeared in that cold snap that followed. Not many apples on the trees come autumn that year!

Anyway, I am glad to be here and happy to take over.

I've got a hot date with the sun. We're meeting at the Equinox about half way's journey for the both of us on the 21st of March. I could use a good dose of heat to warm me through after all that frost and ice you heaved on us this year. What were you thinking?

Freezing cold one minute and rather barmy the next. It makes it rather difficult to control the thermostat; but I guess the decision on how to play things takes place a bit higher up, no?

Anyway, gotta go and get things moving; see you next year!

Love, Spring"

SABRINA DEARBORN, GLASTONBURY

"Dialogue: Winter to Spring

"Winter: "I am so tired. It's been a long hard slog this year and I'll be glad of a rest. Come along, hurry up. My toes are cold and my fingers frostbitten, not to mention the icicles on my nose. Never mind all that, the snowdrops are coming along nicely and there's plenty of daffodil bulbs in store. You'll soon have your hands full with the baby birds and young creatures. You'd better watch out for the Young God. He gets a bit frisky at this time of year.

I do have to go now. You can get on with it and enjoy the sunshine.

Spring replies: Oh well. I suppose you must be going. Thanks for all the hard work you've done looking after the robins and the hibernating snails.

Don't you worry about the Young God. I'll lead him in a merry dance for sure. Of course the new birds and baby animals are so cute, it's not really any trouble looking after them. The Easter bunny can be a bit of a nuisance, but it's only once a year after all.

I won't keep you now. We'll meet again next time. I shall look forward to it"!

PAULINE ROYCE, GLASTONBURY

"A dialogue between Winter and Spring"
    "Winter:
    With my feet in a nailcurling toehold
    I will hold off your coming yet
    Till the warming sun on my head
    Starts melting my firm resolve.
    I know
    My time is slipping away
    You push me into oblivion;
    If merging and meshing,
    Quickly becoming one
    Is the modern thing to do
    That's not who I am:
    My essential nature is darkness
    Holding time and intent in my being
    And the mystery of definite endings
    Yet becoming something anew.
    So hear me you flashy youngster,
    Bloated with urgent new life
    Respect my timely going
    Or suffer my temper's destruction
    You are still a child of my seed
    And mine is the final word.

Spring Back to Winter:
Hey, out of my way Old Man!
I've no time
For slow deliberation
For dragging my feet in the mud.
There are things to be greened
And chicks to be hatched
And all life to be lived in full.
I've got buds to burst,
Rivers to swell
And flowers to help claim their colour
Not for me
The dull shades of winter
Your no-man's-land of blandness;
The light lives in my Soul,
My sister is the Radiant Rainbow
Whose brilliance I use
As a template
For plants
To grow into their own".
INGELISE JENSEN, GLASTONBURY

CHAPTER FIVE: THE SANCTUARY OF YOUR WRITING

"My Special Space for Writing"

"Right now my designated special place has been and is my seat by the window in my lounge. This space draws me to sit here, no matter what I'm doing; writing, reading, watching television.

The window itself draws you to it, a wide bay window letting in the light and the magnificent overview of the Mendips and Cheddar Valley.

Views from this window are amazing, always changing, never the same.

Dawn lights of multi-dimensional oranges to the right of the window is to the East. Sunlight falls sideways over the Mendips at dawn and dusk, showing the recesses of the hills as darker areas whilst the prominent areas are bathed in beautiful light.

Or, like today, this morning with grey mist hanging up through the valley. Does it promise a fine day later or will it stay dismal and give a cold, damp uninteresting day? Who knows. That's the beauty of my window on the world.

To see whitish fluffy clouds skitting up through the valley at eye height to me here, or maybe even lower, and then to see below them smoke from a bonfire that goes the opposite way.

To see the massive Hercules transporter planes that fly through the valley at eye height, see the pilots in the cockpit.

Should I hold my cup up and offer them a cuppa?

The wind blows up here so often, and thanks to next door's flag, I can even see which way the wind blows.

The lights at night are equally fascinating, and bonfire night was a free show all around.

in thinking about a special place to write in, I realize that anywhere I am that the call to write will be special. It is the essence within me that is special, it is me that has the gift and talent within a way I had not imagined or ever thought of, a way to connect with the true essence of me".

DAPHNE GARLAND, GLASTONBURY

"Magical Mercurial Moment"
    "Cafe clamour
    Crowds around.
    Four gathered
    Met together.
    For this moment,
    Though we did not know it.
    As the afternoon passed
    We wrote.

And words sang,
Something so newly arrived
Opening its mouth amongst us.
Finding the phrases
To communicate presence
That's come seeking connection
And the strangest thing
It didn't stay our guest
But shivered through us
Rippling off the paper
Over the tables,
Out through the walls
And into everything".
JACKIE CROVETTO, GLASTONBURY

"When I Meet My Muse"
"When I meet my Muse, I want to be ready.
So I make my bed, take care of the parakeets, fold
The Laundry, make two batches of soy milk, tidy all
The papers on the kitchen counter.

I eat, put away clean dishes, wash dirty
Dishes, start the dishwasher for yet more dishes. I
Shower, catching the cold water to wash my
Underwear, which I hang outside. I fertilize the
Porch plants, and pot up those tiny pine seedlings in
A pot too deep for bonsai but big enough that they
Might sister-grow.

I put a new roll of toilet paper on the spindle
And wipe down the kitchen counters and stove. It
Could go on and on. This is, of course, how I fill
My days, spend down my precious energies, avoid
Writing.

It's also how I center myself, clear the way,
And when the last quotidian task is done I think,
'There, I'm ready. C'mon, Muse, bring it on'!

Sometimes, if Her tasks are done, She does.
JOAN ZERRIEN, IDYLLWILD

CHAPTER SIX: CALMLY RISKY WRITING

"You have to give up the life you have, to get to the life that's waiting for you"

."Open arms inside to a massive sunshine hug. Home beckoning me with

outstretched rays of sunshine.

Laughter employed on wings of sound as I consider what love asks me to do.

Once again give up knowing, don't fear the world and its cacophony of sound. Ordinariness takes an interchange with the mythic.

Pleas of specifics, wholeheartedness entwined with vulnerability.

What is it that I am asked to do live the ordinary from the mythic.

Come forward, stepping lightly across the stones found on the river bed, with water playing round my feet.

Whispers of encouragement: "Follow your heart, follow your heart through the passage of time".

JACQUELINE REDMOND, GLASTONBURY

"I Write With The Belief Of Alchemists"

"I bubble and burble in my retort. I have reached Negredo, that fabulous moment of transition and redemption, the point where lead turns into gold, where the solution clears and a new substance is born.

I was no good in chemistry at school. It didn't relate to

anything, a fragmented clinical environment of separate ingredients and philosophies that never seemed to form a cohesive whole. Where were the maths of Pythagoras? Where was the Golden Mean?

Bubble, bubble toil and trouble. What a toil that time was: hormones flowing, burning desire in my mind and body, my heart like a souped-up racing engine seeking to roar through life for the sheer hell of it and the absolute impossibility of sitting still.

If only I knew then what I know now. That by adding the right ingredients to life, Peace can be had anywhere, and I do mean anywhere! I have sat frozen in lead, the steady inertia of life holding me down and holding me back. I have felt the fire of life racing through me, burning through me like a long slow fuse followed by a massive explosion. I have been a time bomb exploding maniacally in all directions. I will not mix! I will not meld. I will not break down and lose this leaden self, the molten fire.

And then a drop of Love from the Creator. The one who sits outside the retort, outside the lab even, watching this great experiment unfold, a microcosm of all that is on this tiny blue planet.

Plop! A gentle drop and the whole mix changes. Plop.Plop.Plop. the roiling becomes a spiralic movement leading forward what was into a New Life, New Light. A rhythmic dance and the first glimmer, a sparkle from a spark and suddenly the whole solution is clear. There is coolness to balance the fire and an eruption into gold.

> 'make new friends,
> but keep the old,
> one is silver and the other gold'

The lead now silver, the soul now gold".

SABRINA DEARBORN, GLASTONBURY

CHAPTER SEVEN: PORTRAITS OF YOU AND YOUR FAMILY

"Black shoes"

"Black leather shoes in men's size 9, solid and sensible. Specially cleaned on a Saturday night for church on a Sunday morning. The sharp smell of polish being pushed into leather with a small brush and then swished to shine with a larger softer brush.

As my brothers grew, there were more sturdy pairs lined up for the weekly ritual two, three, four, and then the fifth. My shiny patent leather ones were set at the end of the line in time fixing my position in relation to the others and by their very shimmer being that bit different from the rest. While my father cleaned, my brothers would take turns to buff and shine edging into position for their turn.

My mother's Sunday shoes were her own domain. They required cream, not polish. Her range of little pots of coloured creamed matched each pair which, in turn, matched a Sunday outfit.

Colour co-ordination was a keynote and now an echo of those bustling Saturday nights comes to me as I see the dusty maroon and teal green and squirrel grey shoes covered in dust in the bottom of the wardrobe. Matching coats and hats hang above, all unworn for twenty-five years or more but still there because in her 94th year, she sometimes still thinks she might need them one day and that is reason enough not to give them away.

When my father died, one of my brothers took his work clothes and shoes into the garden and burned them, his own funeral pyre to meet the unexpressed pain. In his coffin my father had lain in his one good suit, not filling it anymore of course, and wearing his best shoes, well polished. When someone is going from one world to the next they need to look their best! The work boots that he had worn every day on the farm were left among the Wellingtons' just in case they might fit someone someday.

The thought of someone fitting into my father's shoes one day makes me smile. Too wry a cliché to be ignored.

Have I looked all my life for a man who works a twelve hour day out on the land in his hard-sold boots and then dance the evening away, kicking sparks from the stone flagged floor with hob-nailed shoes? Have I looked for someone who took time to look for the sacred and made sure his family was well-prepared too?

As I slop around in a pair of easy fit sandals of indeterminate colour, I muse that the men I have loved have all had a preference for a good solid leather shoe".

MAGGIE STEWART, GLASTONBURY

"Where I Grew Up and How it Affected Me"

"My first twelve years were spent in the home of my Chinese maternal grandparents on the outskirts of Kuala Lumpur, the capitol of Malaysia.

Amber evenings gave way to sultry tropical nights, often pierced by thunderclaps and torrential rain.

The evening of May 13, 1969, stands out in my memory.

The calm rhythms of the day were permeated by an uncomfortable tension in the air. Earlier on, imams sang their dawn prayers from neighborhood mosques and devotees at Indian temples jingled and clanged their way through the day.

By evening, my extended family of aunts, uncles, cousins and grandparents huddled with myself, my parents and siblings in the lounge room, overseen by a framed picture of Jesus of the cross, legacy of grandfather's Catholicism. Beneath this picture was a plaque showing that Jesus was the unseen guest at every meal.

The sense of tension intensified as the evening wore on, perceptible even to my six-year old sensibility. Hushed conversations revealed there was danger afoot.

'They'll be coming over the hills behind this estate with their parangs (scythes); they've been chopping off heads of Indians in the kampungs (villages)', whispered my uncle, referring to the main ethnic groups, Malays, who were now using force to gain political and economic power in post-colonial Malaysia.

Being of Chinese heritage, we were also targeted as the wealthier cultural group in charge of the nation's big business. By the morning, curfews were in place and many days passed when the school bus didn't arrive to take me to school.

Most of the horror and gore escaped my knowledge until many years later, thanks to being too young to read the newspapers and to my parents being discreet about what was happening. However, I will never forget the fear on their faces and in their bodies as the weeks and months wore on. This fear eventually led my parents to make the decision to emigrate to Australia some years after these events.

Those tense weeks lay the seeds to my acute sensitivity to race issues which would then be compounded by life in predominantly white Australia for the next twenty-two years. Pity really, when the roots of my early childhood were in the multi-racial melting pot that

was and still is the city of Kuala Lumpur. My friends from kindergarten onwards were of a variety of colours, creeds and religions ñ Chinese, Malay, Indian, Eurasian and Caucasian children were my playmates in Malaysia. On weekends, my parents took my siblings and I to the swimming pool at the Regent Hotel where we mingled with white families, expatriates and tourists from Britain, Europe and America.

My favourite pastime for many years was tuning in to short wave radio so that I could listen to news broadcasts from Britain and the USA.

From an early age, I wanted to be a part of the global village that existed in my mind long before the term was coined. While I waited for school buses in the searing tropical heat or lashed by the pelting rain of mid-afternoon tropical thunderstorms, I would escape to far-flung adventures with the Bobbsey twins in cheerful America or the Famous Five and Secret Seven of Enid Blyton's idyllic England. I imagined myself running through heather-covered glens, bluebell and clover-filled meadows, or exploring caves in smugglers coves".

FELICITY DALTON, GLASTONBURY

"Front Porch"

"My father stepped out of the bedroom window in his pajamas and stood on the roof of the front porch.

Overhead the first sputnik flew by silently and changed our world forever. All the images from my brothers' Dan Dare annuals came to life. It was possible to travel to space. We would be going to the moon in no time. It was highly likely that little green men from Mars would visit us soon as we had clearly demonstrated our interest in them with this fantastic invention.

At this time we still had Dolly and Bob. These two large gentle farm horses had been my father's work shires for ten years and more. They had pulled the harrow and plough with a steady rhythm with his guiding hand keeping a straight line. In later years he was to say that getting the first tractor and stopping working with the horses was the biggest change in seventy years of farming. He said he missed their company. The sound of breath on a frosty morning, the clop of hoof kicking hard soil. He missed their reliability every time the tractor broke down. He missed their nuzzling warm quietness.

But my father was a man focused on progress; he would put his name down to go to the moon given half a chance".

MAGGIE STEWART, GLASTONBURY

"Family Portrait"

"I'm looking at two photographs and crying. In the first, I am a six year old girl with a bad haircut and turned-in knees. I'm surrounded by my brother, two sisters, my Mom and Dad. My mom has large eyeglasses and my dad has what looks like a little 'fro.

I look uncomfortable and am twisted around and glaring at my younger sister.

The second photograph shows another family dressed up, two women, two children, a boy and a girl. I look closely at the other woman and smile, the two kids are in between us. The boy is glaring and the girl is grinning widely into the camera. Two of us are light-colored, our children are cinnamon colored. This is my family now.

At six years old I hated my little sister; she blew into my life and was cute and did everything perfectly. I did everything differently and threw tantrums. I couldn't break into the coolness of my older brother's and sister's world. From the moment my younger sister began to share my room we were categorized as the younger ones when all I wanted to do was to play with the older ones. We shared a room covered with zig zag, multi-colored wallpaper; my Mom said it made us crazy. There was a rocking chair in the room. I'd get stuck in it and scream until someone opened the door after they looked in on me during a tantrum. Other times I'd crawl into a drawer or hang out a window, also stuck.

We lived in a rough part of Seattle near the projects. I walked to school each day with my brother and sisters. At our school, teachers were not afraid to discipline the bad kids. I remember Patrick getting tied to his chair in first grade and in second grade; I was lucky not to get my mouth taped shut. We'd all heard about Mrs. Stedman ripping the tape off Kenny, taking part of his lip. The kids I played with at school were all different skin colors but most people were Black or Asian.

By fourth grade my friends were mostly all boys but a United Nations mixture of ethnicities: a Jew, a German, Japanese-American and African-American.

I no longer felt I didn't belong to a group and had my three best friends, Stanley Haruta, Norris Washington and Stanley Hummel. I was 'Sammy Boy', strong and tough on the playground. My fourth grade teacher, Mrs. Kumata, assured me that I was really cool. Though I wasn't Black, I was something - Jewish.

In fifth grade, my parents decided it was time to get us into a school district that hadn't covered the playground with portables and where kids weren't shaken down for money in the bathrooms.

My dad taught at Bellevue, a suburb of Seattle where money was set aside for new and better schools.

Kids from Bellevue were only one shade, white, and celebrated Christmas with lots of new sweaters and great toys. My mom didn't believe in making a big deal out of Chanukah which only happened to fall near Christmas.

We were the only Jews in our neighborhood and our school that I knew about. At the dinner table, our family argued loudly, someone was sent to their room screaming on the way and the television was always going. We talked a lot about the Viet Nam War and Civil Rights. In Bellevue, I went to dinner sometimes at a neighbor kids' home with dads who were engineers. The meals were quiet and the food was divided into neat portions..."

CARLA SAMETH, LOS ANGELES, CALIFORNIA

"Family and Loss"

"Fragments of thoughts, names, and experience lost somewhere longing to be connected again. I'm searching for the thread and cannot find it. I let everything go and smile, breathe. Let the day wash over me until I'm on the shore of a new event.

Somewhere out there is the past or yesterday populated by those gone from me, who knows where. Did they take my real life? Now in a fury of activity I push each moment into the next, straining, feeling the tension in my neck and arms. My knees feel weakened from some silly twist or turn. Perhaps it is the fall I took, ten years ago, in the Coliseum in Rome.

Falling, Drowning. Furious action to propel me to the top, the sunlight, the breath: the peace that does not come at night, the rest that eludes my bones and makes my eyes ache.

Stillness came out of some endless tunnel attached to the turbulent, black hold of my past; things exploding, disintegrating always coming out at the other end in one piece. Slipping through, forcing my way through, grabbing the hand of those near me to drag them through the perilous whatever.

The mountains offer their dark moist comfort; shadows of the trees; clean damp air. Quiet, protected, secretive, a rescue of sorts. The hills embrace me like a mother's arms. The trees on the timberline stand guard like a father and all through the mountains the wind moving like laughter is a sister".

Gale Cohen, LOS ANGELES, CALIFORNIA

CHAPTER EIGHT: "IF THE WALLS HAD EARS"

"If The Walls Had Ears, they would have heard..."

"This writing is from the point of view that walls do have ears. Walls with ears hear stories told to no one else. They are very discreet, those walls. They never betray the secrets and the sigh, the compromises and the lies. I wonder if they blend them in with other stories of a happier nature, little cries of ecstasy, transports of delight, murmurings and mutterings and laughter in the night. Perhaps they wrap themselves in these stories, wear them like lichen and moss, or little strands of fern.

What happens if the walls should be worn down or torn apart someday?

Do the stories drift off into the air, to be retold in distant places in other tongues"?

PAULINE ROYCE, GLASTONBURY

CHAPTER NINE: "WHAT WOULD YOU WANT FUTURE GENERATIONS TO KNOW ONE HUNDRED YEARS FROM NOW"?

"Grandmother"

"Grandmother, what do you think I should know to serve

myself, my people and create a beautiful world?

"I think you should know that life is no picnic. My life in Donegal has been hard but it is the only life I know. I have never travelled far and know the shape of Muckish mountain humpbacked blue against the horizon of my world.

Below it lies the turf bog where we have walked and worked in the soft wet wind listening to the sound of curlews and lapwings calling from the reed beds.

I only have to turn my head and look to the west to see the best sunsets in the world. Scarlet blazing seascapes that only stop at America.Ocean wide and deep, holding the bones of my grand-parents' generation.

I scrape a living here and the work is rough and hard. But at night I gather with the neighbours to hear a tune and tell a tale and feed our souls with good company.

You know the house is not a mile from Fairy Glen. I have tipped my hat to the little folk on my way to Marble Hill strand.

Your father comes from my bones and blood and has been gifted with the glint of laughter in his eyes. My own life was too near the time of the Great Sorrow to allow for much of that. You live in more comfortable times though and although I don't want to see you lazing about, you can go easy on yourself. There is enough of me in you to keep you from becoming idle.

So... remember the sunsets, remember the people long gone, remember the people who want to sit at your hearth and have you sit at theirs.

And remember to tip your hat to the wee folk who are always closer than you think".

MAGGIE STEWART, GLASTONBURY

"What Would You Like to Write For Others One Hundred Years From Now?"

"1908"

"I have sat and thought for a while about the year 1908, but here at the start of my writing and the still new twentieth century, I have no context. My knowledge of history seems suddenly poor, and I can't grasp an event in my mind to act as a jumping off point. I think of old newspapers, black print on a broadsheet of old yellowed paper, no pictures to supplant a thousand words, and I wonder what today's headline might have been all those years ago.

My thoughts turn to my relatives passed, folk I never knew, but whose shape and features or mannerisms I might just recognize as a glimmer of something familiar, perhaps in the mirror. Or a hint of history caught in my mother or father's eye. Did they sit and turn the pages of that paper in the morning? Where were they then? What were they doing? But already, I am taking things for granted. I have an education. Could they even read? Yes, my knowledge of family history also seems impoverished. I really have so little to know them by, the ones that went before.

Mostly, what I do have falls into the realm of family fragments and myth, little leads from stories heard in childhood, and as such I can say very little about what is real or actual. Except that I am now, and so they have been. Yet I find it hard tonight to even contemplate a timeline back to the turn of the century. I work through generations: my life, from parents, of grandparents, and great-grandparents.

My attention is caught by the gaps, the things I can't see, the links I don't make and the questions with answers unknown. I have little knowledge of my paternal grandparents or great-grand-parents; this is largely a hole, a space in the page of personal history. A story cut out of the newspaper and put away, precious, but somehow lost or misplaced in the family tale that unfolded as its sequel. A reminiscence that never quite made it to the scrapbook. So to tell tale of that generation would be a story inked almost entirely from the imagination, with only scant clues left in memory boxes as backstory.

1908: the hangover of a Victorian hierarchy and a life in service to the richer classes. A glass-beaded cushion; a time of lives still held together by the rigid stitches and social mores of a class-filled society, fragile perhaps, with scandal to come. A world where revolutions were starting to turn, and where the cloud of war would soon condense into a cold rain. Postcards home, and correspondents' words washed off paper in the miserable holes of the European trenches, where lives were cut out, like so many stories from the daily papers, leaving only spaces that were never really filled".

STACEY CAMFIELD, GLASTONBURY

CHAPTER TEN: CELTIC WRITING TODAY
"A place where I have been which is calling me"

"Today I walked out on the levels ñ high dry grasses flagging their shaggy tops in unison. Dark waters rippling under the sweep of chill wind. My footsteps sank into the black damp earth leaving shallow imprints of toe and heel, toe and heel. Swans nesting on loose piles of dry reed exposed to the watcher in this most precious exercise. An occasional lift and slap of heavy wing as heavy bodies heaved from the Water.

I drew my shawl closely around me and knew that I had walked this way before. Reaching for the brittle shells of broken reed stalk, I felt in the memory of my fingers the sinew of coarse reed thread stripped for weaving. The rawness of chilled wet hands working the wet fibres in a mix of rush and nettle to bulk the garment's growth.

We, the women of the wetlands, worked our daily rhythm with the flight of the birds. Tern and teal, moorhen and finch crisscrossed our days with sound and direction.

Deep throated croaking drew us to fresh feeding grounds. Bird and people, hunters all, we followed the nesting routes as the seasons passed overhead and made our new homes at the water's edge.

At the time of full moon and Spring tide the sharp tang of sea washed gently over the levels bringing distant worlds quietly to our door".

MAGGIE STEWART, GLASTONBURY

"About Samhain"
    "Our lives
    Spiralling inwards
    Downwards
    From the dizzy heights of summer
    And outer-focus
    Of to-ing and fro-ing
    Between people,
    Relations, actions,
    Now giving way,
    Releasing its grip on me
    To let me follow
    My seasonal rhythm
    Of down and out
    Inwards and downwards
    The black hem of Samhain's skirt
    Just visible,
    Swirling at the edge
    Of the spiral
    As I follow
    The Deadening pace
    downwards,
    inwards,
    somehow relishing

the blindness
of dying to the outer world
as I pursue
the relentless path
taking me back
into my seeding ground
to meetings along the way
with the Grandmothers
of the seed
from which I came, who
wove a shawl of blood
around me -
warm, dark, comforting
growing material
in which I grew
into the "I"
That is Me".
INGELISE JENSEN, GLASTONBURY

"The Irish Bridge"

"The tiny bridge over a stream was turned by the curve of the
road so that the stone walls stood, not parallel to each other, but
angled, randomly owning their own side of the narrow wayside.

Each stone edged by the speckle and spread of hard grey
green mosses. Fringes of acid yellow lichen mapping out the lie of
another land. A land only visible when you are not looking.
Between the cracks chinks of pink and purple glint and tease.

A stone spider swings in a loop of wild tension and links again
to dry surface.

Slick shine touch from ten thousand fingertips have surfaced
the top rock into smoothness now. Shelf for elbows, saddle for
striding, seat for just sitting.

When you throw two twigs into the water the flow whisked
your laughter to the other side of the road as, crashing against the

wall, the rocket or flying fish came flushing from the dark mouth below. Stream swift.

Like all turns in the road, twists of water, or curve of overhanging tree this bridge once had its given name. From a time when people had a true relationship with the small places and named them in keeping with their essence.

After the English came to Ireland and remapped the land and its people, this bridge had no name".

MAGGIE STEWART, GLASTONBURY

"Longing, love, labyrinth"
   "The sea is silent
   So far below
   And I want to be part
   Of a wholeness
   Where I belong,
   Have belonged
   And will always belong.
   On this Cornish Coast
   Two were born here
   Many times before.
   I long for the way
   Things were when
   I walked on the beach
   And a flock of seagulls
   Rose before me
   Into the sky".
   ALICIA ROWE, RIVERSIDE, CALIFORNIA

CHAPTER ELEVEN: THE COLLECTIVE WORLD VOICE
"Memories of a Courageous Woman"

"Mama Rose, it's a long time that I've desired to write our story. I say ours, because it's really about the time we spent together, our sharing and caring. Short though it was, its part of

an everlasting memory of the great women of Tanzania who
have touched my life.

The name Rose says a lot. I'm not sure why you chose it. We
should have called you Mama Vitalia, the name of your first-born,
but that never happened....

Could I guess then? Give you the name I feel you would have
chosen?

'Aliyepewa mwanga na huangaa '(she who received light and
enlightens),'aliye na

amani '(she who is at peace), 'aliyeshinda '(she who has won).I
could go on....

I remember the first time we met. You were seated on a bike,
that swollen knee dangling hideously from it. I wondered how far
you'd come and how you'd survive the pain. You didn't tell me
the whole truth at once, but gradually I came to know. I guessed
right away that this was something pretty bad, but I hoped, as so
many times before, that I was wrong.

Luckily the doctor from the mission hospital was coming in a
couple of days. I couldn't bear sending you on a useless trip to the
local hospital where you would have found no help anyway. You
agreed you'd wait, so Sister Jane took you home and said she'd
pick you up on that day. We found you lived only seven miles
away, and so I knew how long your agony had been.

The doctor confirmed my feeling. It was something that could
not be healed; it had gone way too far. Just keep you out of pain,
he said. So I gave you something for the pain, and promised you
and myself that I'd look for something more. I told your husband.
I trusted him... I was to regret that much in a time not far away.

I counted the days, searched for the pills, and then a moment
after work one day I headed for your home... We had a nice chat
in the beginning... and then you challenged me: "Why didn't the
doctor send me to the hospital?" you asked, "my knee looks
pretty bad."

I held my breath, trying to think fast, for it's forbidden in your culture to tell the person these kinds of things. But your eyes were saying you wanted the truth. And so I trusted you, and myself, and told you what I knew.

You didn't ask how long you'd live. Living had taught you that life is always in God's hands. Modern science hasn't changed that a lot.

You seemed peaceful, strong, when I left you that evening.

I did not sleep much that night. I wondered if you were facing this alone, no human touch to soothe the pain.

I came only later to know that your husband didn't want what was now to him a useless wife. He said it at the local pub and you came to know. But it would be another day that you would cry on my shoulder and tell me so.

I came to know your children, all girls: Vitalia, the first-born, and Lukia, your last-born. You loved them so and somehow it seems that this was to be the greatest part of your pain, leaving them to the unknown.

I found you crying one day. Your daughters needed a mother. After all, they were only five, seven and ten years old. You felt so bad that they, instead, had to take care of you.

When I complained about your husband not helping you or the girls, you told me something of your marriage and your husband. You hadn't wanted to be his second wife. You'd run away, but the bride price had already been paid and in the end you had to go. A bride price usually guarantees you'll be taken care of. I objected. So what happened after that?

I came to know him better at the same time as I came to know Lukia better in a new way. The five-year old had managed to outwit her dad.. It is a shame things have to be that way. He'd come the afternoon before and started harvesting the corn from the field you and your daughters had cultivated on your own. He really had no claim to it, even if you had been well. Your eyes flashed anger and wry humour as you went on telling this story. No protest moved him and he took it all way before evening, appearing to enjoy doubly what he had done.

He hadn't counted on Lukia though. Shed watched him and knew where he had taken it. When all were asleep that night she went out and slowly hauled it all back. You knew what shed done, but not where shed hidden it. She didn't want you to have trouble. Luckily, for once at least, he was ashamed enough not to take the case to the elders. You were proud of your daughter, I remember. You had hope for her future then, whatever would happen.

I took you and the girls one Saturday to Kibao. Mama Jane came to help me load you and your things into the car. Your mom had agreed to come and help, too. The girls were excited about the trip... You sat in the back of the Land Rover.

You seemed to be in deep thought, or was it prayer? As I waited to load something else in the back, I dared ask you what your thoughts were. I'm forever glad I invaded your privacy.

I thought you'd say, "I'm wondering if I'll see my home again, or I wonder if I'll die in Kibao,. or something similar. But, no, I couldn't have guessed. You said, "If I weren't sick the blind woman and her two children would be living with us at this time of year. I wonder now what they will do".

You left me breathless.

I went to see the blind woman on Christmas Eve. I didn't sleep all night. But that's another story.

I only saw you once at Kibao. You were doing better, even if the growth was thriving too... What did I hear about you that day? Did anyone ever tell you? I know I never got the chance.

You'd become a wise woman, I'd been told. Not that you were aware of it. But men (unusual!) and women of different ages, tribes and creeds were knocking on your door, to talk to you, listen to you, just drink in the joy and peace that radiated in your space. I remember, too, how often the young women who worked with me would want to come along to visit you. There was more than pity there. There was admiration, respect, wonder, at how you could be as you were.

I was far away when you died. You had a nice funeral, I heard, and were buried near your home.

Nothing of your specialness appeared. Your daughters, too, disappeared soon after. Where have they gone? No one seems to know.

Yet your memory lives on, in so many of us whose lives you've touched, and whose lives have never been the same. I know because I've heard. But most of all because I can touch the very part of me that was once and still is a part of you".

SANDY DEMANN, IDYLLWILD, CALIFORNIA

"The Spiral Path"
"As my hesitant feet
Seek out the steps
Hidden in the moonless dark,
The trace of that Ancient Path
Faintly starts taking form;
Slowly it fills out all around me
In space
In ground
And within me
The wet leafy smells fill my nose
The dankness swelling my eyes
And tweaking my heaving guts.
Alarmed, I wonder where I have landed
Is it safe to be in this place?
Mind-fear starts taking hold,
Looking for routes to normality
Out of this multi-dimensional world.
But heart remains steady, only just
Here, choice is not an option
As it was then
In that far-away time

Before my eyes had learnt
To see the world from within,
To know
The inner side of the world
And the vastness of Her realm,
Her presence is strong, unmistakable
Old Mother of the Deep
The power of Her Place
Is immediate
The potent stillness
Shrinking,
The veils of the Worlds

I sense the gently curving steps
Pointing to downwards and inwards,
Feel the Path weaving through me
And suddenly I know
That we're One:
The Path I chose as my task
In that far-away time
When my soul-eyes were learning to see

Now the opening
Of that spiral path downwards,
Calls me
To descend once again;
But now I know
That the Path
Is more than something to follow;
At once
It is both the beginning
Of that journey
Into the depths,
As well as the place of endings

Where the silence of the Mothers
Give nurture
In what's been seeded
In the space given over
From the old dying out."
INGELISE JENSEN, GLASTONBURY

CHAPTER TWELVE: FROM ISOLATION TO UNIVERSAL SHARING: THE DIVINE FEMININE CIRCLE

Writing from Sacred Site Tours to England from West Coast of United States

"The Chalice Well, Glastonbury: My first visit"

"So much happened before I could step into the garden.

John turned the van from busy Chilkwell Street into the Chalice Well driveway much later in the day than we had planned. The four of us dragged out our suitcases, but Jan couldn't find her luggage. We hovered around, checking and rechecking the boot, under seats, on the driveway. John strolled happily down the lane toward us. He had carried the large suitcase up to St Michael's, the cottage where we'd be staying.

Then Deanne and I both wanted the same room, Rowen, with its window overlooking the back garden. Every shade of green echoed in the landscape. We verbally tussled for possession until a rabbit searching for dinner near the potting shed diverted our attention.

I suggested we meditate and that would help us decide. We sat on opposite sides of the bed. Immediately I realized that the room was hers; she never thought otherwise.

As the others finished unpacking, I slipped out the back door and wound my way through St Michael's gate and past the garden's information booth. Maybe coming to Glastonbury wasn't a good idea. Maybe I'd lived too long with the shimmering vision of Avalon and no reality could match that.

With my head down and hands in my pockets, I headed for the trees. It was dusk and the damp grass squished under my tennis shoes. I stopped when I felt as if someone had addressed me. Across the grass, the yew trees felt welcoming, so welcoming I wanted to cry and I ran to meet them.

I was very happy to be back as if I'd lived here before. The trees, the grass, the entire garden felt so Alive. With my arms out, I twirled around three or four times until a lovely dizziness slowed me down.

That's when I sensed them, the elementals or "fairies." No, it wasn't just the dizziness nor was it a definite meeting like with the yews.

Breathing deeply, I quieted myself and stood still. Something was just out of reach. If I could see better, there'd be small, sparkling energetics flying and dancing around me.

My three companions called from the stairs leading to the lower level of the garden. I quickly walked over.

One by one, as if in a processional, we quietly descended to the Vesica Piscis pond to start the evening ritual we had planned.

Now the four of us sit in St Michael's cozy living room writing and reading our writing to each other. I choose not to remember that I have a demanding life somewhere else, for here, for this brief time at the Chalice Well, my inner and my outer lives can be the same. My energy can blend into the energetic of the place. I've touched a home, and I relax in that reunion.

I happily allow the Chalice Well magic to wrap its web around me and I, who love freedom beyond all else, acquiesce to its charms".

SUSAN HECHT, LAKE FOREST, CALIFORNIA

"My Tree on the Abbey Grounds, Glastonbury"

"Her name is Glynnis of Ynis Witrin. She speaks inside my

mind and invites me to enjoy her shade and the cool breeze. Glynnis drops a leaf for me somewhere. "Look for it" she says. Here it is between my knees on the green grass and greener clover. I find another leaf from Glynnis. First one is brown, second green with gold and sienna specks.

And now I pick up a red hawthorn berry and now a third leaf. I tuck the small trio of her leaves carefully between my journal pages.

I love drawing leaves and trees. My most memorable drawing made at elementary school in Mrs. Shaver's first grade class was a marvelously big maple tree.

Mom tacked it to the back porch wall at our home and there it stayed until the fragile newsprint paper disintegrated.

I want to rush out and buy crayons now. I feel five and a half years old just now.

Chris 5.5, Grade 1 artist.

I'm time traveling. It was fifty years ago that I drew the big beautiful tree, a drawing that haunts my mind until today. What is it about being here in Glastonbury, dear Avalon, in which there is no linear time? I truly feel like I'm fifty years in the past.

I miss my Mommy and I'm crying big tears. In the present moment I'm ok, knowing I can easily access this Avalon consciousness from anywhere.

The Tree, I touch her rough bark, which had deep lines, texture running in broken horizontals. Hers is thick fragrant bark with grey green lichen adorning her gnarly trunk and a few leaves on short steams growing out of the burly base like feathers at her ankles.

She is a beauty, dancing as she leans into the west. I do her portrait with my Holga camera, and sketch her trunk in my journal. After I pick up gifts of her leaves I water her with my tears as I lean against her bark. 'I'll see you later tonight, Glynnis Witrin and bring the Goddesses to meet you'.

I hear you invite me to bring a tiny klootie to place in your

sacred branches. Yes, that I will do with joy".
CHRISTINE LOUISE EAGON, VANCOUVER,
WASHINGTON

"A Glastonbury Memory"
"We live by the sun.
We feel by the moon.
We move by the stars.

The moon, the moon, the great glorious moon that graced our
mountain last weekend, pouring its liquid light through the
windows above my bed, bathing my head and hair, my sleeping
eyes, my cheeks, throat and heart in its full moon brilliance.
Bringing me back to Idyllwild, grounding me in the sweet, pine
scented air that I've come to love so much, welcoming me home
from my journey across the sea, to wet, wild and wonderful
England, where for seven long days we sloshed through puddles,
squelched in mud, and made ourselves comfortable in the soft
misty gray of early morning, on lush damp grass, our backs
supported by ancient, lichen covered stones, while the world
came slowly alive beneath us.

If Idyllwild in June is dry and silky, then Somerset is bursting
with wetness, running with fountains, springs and waterfalls,
gardens exploding in a riot of purple, reed, orange and green.
After a week of nearly continuous rain, the clouds finally part and
the low, dark and threatening night sky began to shimmer with
the light of a thousand stars, while the sliver of a new moon made
its way gracefully across the rooftops of Glastonbury".
BRONWYN JONES, IDYLLWILD, CALIFORNIA

"A Blessing"
"I descended the steep slippery steps holding to the unsteady
rail and found myself at their end surrounded by high vertical

walls of growing green on dark rock.

I stood before the magnificence of the falls of St. Nectan's Glen.

I was alone yet felt a tangible presence in this sacred place. There were pictures, candles, pieces of cloth, poems and small statues carefully laid in the rock crevices and on the ledges. Had this place offered others something out of respect so they had left something of themselves here?

I had nothing to offer except perhaps a coin. I opened my purse and started to take out a fifty pence piece. No, I must offer something of greater value. I took out the largest one I had, a one pound coin.

I walked out on the piled up rocks that formed a damp pathway to the center of the steam. I felt a stunned sense of awe at the unique beauty and power before me and a true connection with all those had stood here in reverence and respect. I tossed the coin up through the center of the opening into the rushing water.

I stood in prayerful silence and as I did some of the foaming water suddenly splashed up onto my face. As if in a blessing, a blessing from St Nectan".

VEDA ROUBIDEAUX, IDYLLWILD, CALIFORNIA

"Water Workshop"
   "Standing solemn and silent
   in a circle of pilgrims
   at Chalice Well
   The wind blows my hat off,
   Floats if playfully and
   Lets it land, big as a dinner plate,
   On the fountain.
   "Don't be so serious",
   The wind whispers,
   "This is fun".
   ALICIA ROWE, RIVERSIDE, CALIFORNIA

"Missing Nevern"

"Last year I met the Maglocumus Stone in Nevern, Wales. It stands in a churchyard surrounded by centuries' old yew trees, the original sanctuary, embracing, comforting, mysterious and solid.

This year I returned to visit it again only to have my plans change.

All you can do is count on change. Learn to love it.

I am at this moment in the monastic ruins of St David's Cathedral down the road from Nevern. I'm surrounded by tall weathered walls, bright blue sky, buttercups, dime-sized daisies, chattering birds and the greenest grass.

Ancient Spring Renewed.

I was supposed to be somewhere else, but old stones can speak the quiet language across space and time.

The stone at Nevern speaks in Latin and Ogham and Spirit, subconscious stories and secrets.

I'm in love with the Maglocumus Stone just a few miles away. I'm sending my prayers, thoughts, and questions in that direction. I know my vibrations reach the stone.

Are we only meant to meet just once?

What is it you should teach and I should learn?

When I remember you, do you remember me?

What is this affair all about?

No matter where I am, I'll love your more. We share the same source. I sit here in these ruins of St David's close to you and far away at the same time:

The Crone and the Stone.

As I age, like the stone, I will gather wisdom, silence, grace, patience, compassion and the ability to let go. Letting go of the ego, the physical. The outcomes of events are what they are. Moving on, not giving into disappointment or loss.

The stone and the Earth Mother fill my spirit; and my heart is full of love and a little longing. Does the stone long for me? Only

in the wisest way".
  NANCY JOHNSON, LONG BEACH, CALIFORNIA

"Three Kinds of Time"
  "There is real time
  Then there is psychic time
  Like the waves of a sprinkler
  Over the Greenwich Green
  And finally there ís
  GMT
  Which our friend Michou calls
  'Glastonbury Maybe Time.'
  ALICIA ROWE, RIVERSIDE, CALIFORNIA

"AMPLIFIED"
  "Did you notice
  The birdcalls are
  Louder in England?
  They sound like they come
  Through a megaphone,
  Like a mimic exaggerating.
  Do the robins take
  Deeper breaths?
  Back home we'd think
  That trumped up birdcall
  Was an Indian scout
  Alerting His partner
  Before a raid".
  ALICIA ROWE, RIVERSIDE, CALIFORNIA

Writing Number One
  "If you were to begin a pilgrimage,
  "What would be your first step?"
  "Take it in, the traveler, the tree, the breath, the green,

The moist , the misty, the pounding pulse of this place,
Unknown to me and calling me here.

I'll just show up and visit with whatever
Or whoever else
Is called to show up, too.

Will I take it home with me? Will I invite it to stay?
In some way make it last longer than this moment?
The beauty, the ache, the thrill, the throb, the quiet, the
    encounter?

Taking it in, in a moment, is easy;
Caressing it and letting it transform me is not so easy.

Therein is my risk
To be ready to become the me I do not know.

I long for me and fear me all at once.
I anticipate the journey with the excitement of who I will find,
    and
The hope I will return from this labryrinth a new form".
CAROL HIGGINS, RIVERSIDE, CALIFORNIA

Writing Number Two:
    "What was the most valuable moment from yesterday?"
    Most valuable? This is a question that is so difficult to answer.
    For me, things generate and percolate for some time before
    I discover how valuable they are.

    I am trying to be fully present to each moment
    And fully encounters each person.
    I am thinking about meeting the Glastonbury women:
    Larraine, Ingelise, Caroline, Carole, Jacqui, Sabrina,

A special web of connection that vibrates with energy. These
    women
Were so welcoming and fun.
They are valuable to me...

And my little spider in the well, who peeked at me to tell me
    that
The web of creativity is alive in my life;
Just sit and wait for the time to be, or move, or not.

Valuable to attend and be present to quiet and green;
And meet Mr.Ark and Mary in the garden
And soak in the rain and flowers and bees there.
Valuable to drink of the waters that flow unceasing red and
    white.

Most valuable in a most valuable day in a most valuable place
    in a most
Valuable time of a most valuable lifetime".
CAROL HIGGINS, RIVERSIDE, CALIFORNIA

"St. Nectan's Glen"
    "The fairies dance, but I don't see them.
    They laugh behind their hands at me.
    I missed them dancing on the moor
    And in the caves at sea.
    Then I went upon a quest
    To St. Nectan's Glen
    And there upon the waterfall,
    I looked and looked again;
    And coming down upon a cloud
    Of lacy froth so white
    A band of fairies flew
    And blew their flutes with all their might!

'Was that a vision'? I asked Barry,
'Can I believe it's true?'
He twinkled at me and replied,
'That is up to you".
ALICIA ROWE, RIVERSIDE, CALIFORNIA

Chapter 12 (continuation) The Glastonbury Writers

"To enter the darkness where this wound is, will we not be
   shown a true way to serve it?"
From a dream, inspired by Inanna's Return:
"She is coming
Riding on a point of Light
Ever increasing
In volume, it's bright
She's returning,
From where?
Do we even realize
She was absent?
Adapting as we do
To the prevailing powers
That shape us,
Which shaped Her
Into submission
And kept her light
Underground
She is arriving
Out of the black hole
Blunting the sharp edges
Of my senses,
Blurring sight
Muffled ear,
Making mockery
Of my need to make sense,

Of life from the inside.
What is in and what is out?
No landmarks
In this dark and silent world
Why am I here?
Does time still move on, giving hope?
While here, I become Immoveable
In this place of no-doing
And forgetfulness
Of what brought me here in the first place:
My own intent
To find again
The tiny point of light
Shining out of darkness
On which She rides
Into life
New Life".
INGELISE JENSEN, GLASTONBURY

"I said to me, Go Forward!"

"I said to me, go forward! Now is the time to go forward. We cannot return to who we were.

Looking back, my eyes form pillars of salt. For we have lived, and years bring pain.

But now is the time to go forward. Maybe not dancing, my child can do that.

I will walk. I will stride boldly with strength and conviction, purpose, direction.

No longer a child and a dreamer, a butterfly, delighting, but frail.

Now I am a woman, and Priestess and Goddess and Mother. I have tasted the fruit of the tree. I have crawled in misery on the earth. I have given birth in pain and moaning. I have toiled for my daily bread, felt life and death and seen beyond.

So now I am taking this next step. Forward".
PAULINE ROYCE, GLASTONBURY

CHAPTER THIRTEEN: BRINGING THE SOUL BACK HOME:

"Writing Exercises for the Highest Self"

"Stonehenge Prelude"

Cold stone.

Huge blocks of rough hewn solid rock.

First chiseled by molten mass, earth ís core, spewn to the
surface

When the primordial world was coalescing into continents

As the earth spun young and fiery in the universal sky.

Mankind emerged eons later.

What did they see in these megaliths of stone

That spurred them to move them to a flat cold plain

And raise them high and ring them in a circle

And crown their tower tops with horizontal blocks?

Who were these creators, ancient artists of the mist?

What will the stones say to me

When I stand in their presence?

Will I hear them whisper to the wind,

Or will there be profound silence?

Will the thousands of nights that have passed

Since legend flourished

Fall away when I behold them?

I want to touch the stones, to feel

That solidity of the past, the Earth, the Ages.

I long to smell the dampness of ten thousand years

Condensed in the rock crevices

And explore the memory of the Ancients.

I want to see a rainbow, if only in my heart,

And to believe that I have returned again,

Not just visiting for the first time.

We seek the Merlin's magic,
Not wishing to believe we are complete as we are.
It is up to us to produce the greatest magic
Of making our lives whole.
There is no line to cross over,
No bridge to Avalon.
King Arthur lived and died, as we must, too.
With sword of pen
We stroke through the enemy of time,
The villain of complacency,
The warlord of fear,
The throne of self doubt
and strive for self fulfillment.
The Grail, the Chalice that heals all
Is what humankind has sought thorough out the ages.
An elixir, a pot of gold, a fountain of youth.
Yet these are the elements of our being,
The elixir of life, the cup of communion blood
Runs through the veins of us all.
The pot of gold is the fortune we all possess,
Whether it is defined in family, friends or good health.
The fountain of youth is our spirit never to give up.
To know that giving is not taking away".
JAN HARRIS, VAN NUYS, CALIFORNIA

"Stonehenge in the Inner Circle"

"There was an intense intimacy with the stones, with myself and my cold fingers that I tried to protect but to no avail.

Even as they became blanched white and I held the fear of the discomfort to come I did not want to leave the stones.

I was told to bring something to lay upon one of the huge stones to invoke the power it held that I might bring it with me as I left.

A small medallion necklace is what I brought to offer. As I

came into the circle one of the stones called to me, .saying, 'Lay it here'

This I did and waited. After a while I was told 'You may now take it'. I did so and followed the next instruction given. 'Put the medallion on'.

And I did.

Thus I began my time among the stones. My hands huddled into mittens pulled back into sleeves of my jacket for protection. I walked the inner circle several times. Then the outer circle several times.

I did not want to sit and write as some did. I wanted to walk with definite, honorable, seeking steps among these ancient stones.

I stopped at times seeing a chance to capture on film a companion communing with a stone of choice, and then I walked again.

My fingers now very cold and turning quite white. Still, I did not want to leave.

I wonder if this medallion does now hold some power that the deepest part of me perceives and will effect and perhaps will change me.

Have I indeed taken with me something this powerful circle of stones has offered to others and now has offered to me"?

VEDA ROUBIDEAUX, IDYLLWILD, CALIFORNIA

"Circle Lines of Stonehenge and Avebury"

"The Ancient Architect did round
The sacred circle
Stones on mound
To hallow ground
That could contain the mystery.

Could earth encompass

What soul has found?

We place our hopes
With hearts held round
Inside the earth
So boldly crowned,
A misty veil, a whispered sound,
A moon that's new and silvery
Will light my way,
Where yet to be.

Though mystery still shrouds this place,
A benediction Crowns my face.

I step outside the labyrinth,
Awash with ley line energy.

My heart and spirit dance
Spritefully,
Stirred high in ancient
Symmetry".
CAROL HIGGINS, RIVERSIDE, CALIFORNIA

"Words for One World"
    Foreword
    Onward
    Anticipation, no longer waiting
    Expectation
    Emancipation
    Words for
    One world
    Conscious, we are claiming
    Elevation
    Co-Creation

Streaming
Dreaming
Stories teaming, no longer taming
Desire
Destiny

You are for me, and I am for you
Naked, Frightened, Triumphant, Roaring
We call out across ages
We tumble back
True

Love is a word, Hate is too
Write them down. I want them to stare back at you
Beginnings are Defiant of Endings
Circular, Necessary
Illusions on the page

One Door
Closes Another Chapter
Ends
One Heart
Opens Another story
Begins

In whispers
In rapture
In essence
In truth
I only want to be at peace with you

Words for
One world
Conscious, we are claiming

Elevation
Co-creation
Naming ourselves as what we do".
STACEY CAMFIELD, GLASTONBURY

"Tor Walk"
"Climbing up through the sense-numbing greyness
Of mist filling up eyes and nose,
I lose my earthbound bearings
Float about in the nothingness of grey
Only my feet, undeterred
Keep on pushing upwards –
And I barely notice the shift
Opening the Ancient Way:
I suddenly emerge at the top
Into another place –
A world of brilliant light
Expanding above the mists –
Into endless vistas of pure white cloud,
A gently rippling sea of illuminated white
Flowing into eternity.
From the distant world of humanity
The cry of duality dissolves
In the all-pervasive silence of light
Uniting all in One

Another shift –
The Dragon hidden in Wearyall's Land
Slowly appears
Through the soft white rolls of eternity
Spine and long tail arched
In a birthing burst of effort
To pierce the Veil of Separation
Between the Worlds –

Feet deeply anchored in one
Body birthing into the other,
You Ancient Being straddling the worlds
Thus holding the promise of Oneness for us all,
To you I call:
Let us be Walkers
Of the Sacred Land
With love unveiling
The lost secrets
Of the Light in the Earth:
Spirit in Matter.
Dimensions realigned and
Balance restored
We will walk your promise
Into new emergence".
INGELISE JENSEN, GLASTONBURY

"Fire"

Fire is the sign of life, existence, vibration,
creation.
Fire is the burning sensation for the beloved, use it
wisely and it will burn
all your desires.
Fire is a sacred thing, very few know how to use it.
Follow your intuition; fire will surely guide you to
your destination".
AFSANEH AJANG, LOS ANGELES, CALIFORNIA

BOOKS

O is a symbol of the world, of oneness and unity. In different cultures it also means the "eye," symbolizing knowledge and insight. We aim to publish books that are accessible, constructive and that challenge accepted opinion, both that of academia and the "moral majority."

Our books are available in all good English language bookstores worldwide. If you don't see the book on the shelves ask the bookstore to order it for you, quoting the ISBN number and title. Alternatively you can order online (all major online retail sites carry our titles) or contact the distributor in the relevant country, listed on the copyright page.

See our website **www.o-books.net** for a full list of over 500 titles, growing by 100 a year.

And tune in to myspiritradio.com for our book review radio show, hosted by June-Elleni Laine, where you can listen to the authors discussing their books.

MySpiritRadio